DIVORCE: THE CURE THAT KILLS THE PATIENT.

MARRIAGE: IT'S NOT MAGIC. YOU HAVE TO MAKE IT WORK.

HOW NOT TO SPLIT UP is about changing your life...*without* changing partners. Not advice but practical *methods* of dealing with money, careers, sex, fights, children, leisure, travel, apartment living and one hundred and one other of the delightful and disturbing "problem areas" that make living together today's most intimate adventure.

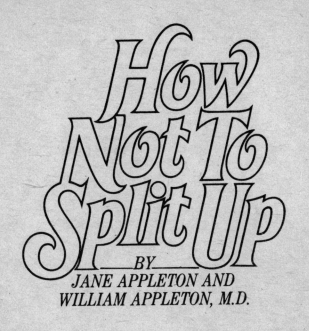

How Not To Split Up

BY
JANE APPLETON AND
WILLIAM APPLETON, M.D.

BERKLEY BOOKS, NEW YORK

Grateful acknowledgment for the quotation on page 83
is made as follows:
"I Wish I Were in Love Again,"
by Lorenz Hart and Richard Rodgers,
copyright © 1937 by Chappell & Co., Inc.
Copyright Renewed. International Copyright Secured.
All Rights Reserved.
Used by permission.

This Berkley book contains the complete
text of the original hardcover edition.
It has been completely reset in a type face
designed for easy reading, and was printed
from new film.

HOW NOT TO SPLIT UP

A Berkley Book / published by arrangement with
Doubleday and Company, Inc.

PRINTING HISTORY
Doubleday edition published 1978
Berkley edition / September 1979
Third printing / July 1981

ISBN: 0-425-05319-9

A BERKLEY BOOK ® TM 757,375
Berkley Books are published by Berkley Publishing Corporation,
200 Madison Avenue, New York, New York 10016.

PRINTED IN THE UNITED STATES OF AMERICA

To Amy, Lucy, and Bill

*Special thanks to Lindy Hess
for her patient guidance.*

CONTENTS

INTRODUCTION

WE HAVE BEEN married for almost twenty years. In our sophisticated university community, this makes us an anachronism. Our three children come home from school and tell us half the class has divorced parents. They joke about us, Mr. and Mrs. How-Not-to-Split-Up. They laugh but we wonder. Are we missing something?

Not immune to the fashions around us, we wonder if we are being lazy in remaining tied to the same person. If we really cared about finding ourselves and establishing intense, deep personal relationships, wouldn't we bid each other a fond farewell and try to find someone new and exciting? Are we too dependent or just apathetic? Are we indifferent to the thrill of getting progressively closer to someone? Have we, alas, given up the hope of finding "love"? Do we perhaps suffer existential despair and have we now resigned ourselves? Is a long marriage a resignation or an affirmation?

We wonder.

It's no wonder we wonder! All around us the Sanctity of Marriage is fluttering helplessly: nobody but nobody is waving that outmoded banner. Divorce is the standard. More and more it is put into a *positive* light. For previous generations, marriage was the answer; for this generation, it is definitely the question. The marital team is the underdog, with no cheerleaders on the sidelines and no fans in the stands. Matrimony is the winter, summer, fall, spring of adult discontent; an emotional vitamin deficiency preventing growth and self-realization. The cure, the tonic, the "pep" pill for this lingering malady is—divorce.

The Sanctity of Separation. You split in order to grow; to find a new relationship, closer and more meaningful than the old one; to realize yourself as a person and, not so nobly, to trade up to someone better. Growth and self-realization are the key words. If you feel locked out of life's wonderful playroom in which satisfyingly single or perfectly mated men and women are romping, why not use those key words to get out of your marriage and into that rec room? Who's or what's to stop you? One by one, time-honored bastions against divorce have fallen—religion, society, law, and family. If your pastor, priest, or rabbi hasn't already hung up his frock and left his flock to find *himself*, he might even give you reasons why you *should* separate. If you talk to your friends, in the name of "friendship" they might deliver the final blow to weakened marital bonds. Talk to your financial and legal advisers. Will they help you stay together? Maybe, or they'll figure out the best (cheap) way to divorce and settle property. Talk to your parents. You might be amazed to discover they too are no longer shocked by divorce—as a matter of fact, they may be contemplating it themselves.

Divorce. And then what? Growth, self-realization? Happiness? The overwhelming relief in shedding the tight skin of responsibility and sensuously slithering in a creative garden of eternal Eden? Not very likely, not according to statistics. *The Gay Divorcee?*—only in movies. Ginger Rogers high-stepping with Fred Astaire on the silver screen is a far cry from the real woman who floundered through multiple marriages. There is nothing "gay" about breaking up a home, a family, an accustomed way of life. Divorce is pain. Increasingly easy to say, easy to do, according to the overwhelming majority of divorced persons, but still a jolting, hideous experience with unpleasant and often unexpected consequences.

Expect, for instance, to lose your powers of concentration, to find yourself unable to function properly in a crowd, and unwilling and unused to being alone. Once your partner, your security is gone, expect to turn to other securities, among them drink and senseless promiscuity. Expect to give over as much as four years of your life to making an "adjustment." All the creative energies to be magically released when *you* were on your own will be just as squandered in your single state as they were in your married one, and there is no longer anyone to blame.

As for "finding yourself," the naïve belief that the Real You is poised behind an imaginary arras, waiting to waltz out à la Astaire and Rogers the minute independence from your spouse is declared, is ridiculous.

Unfortunately, the ideas of mystical change, of growth and self-actualization coming out of divorce are fostered by the proliferation of simple-minded psychologies in practice and in print. The sinister "How To's" with their offbeat upbeat promises make everything seem possible.

"How To"—no matter what the problem, we are bombarded with advice and the word is "communication." Private thoughts and private parts have become public property as people are urged to "reveal" themselves. Break down the barriers and let the world know how you feel. "I think, therefore I am" has been updated to "I am, therefore I must say what I think." Your husband drinks too much? Tell him. Your wife talks too much? Tell her. Your friends ask too much? Tell them. Your dog barks too much? Smack him. Whoever or whatever is bothering, pleasing, teasing, or hurting you is to be notified *immediately*.

Restraint? Quaint. Everyone is racing to the podium opening their self-help books to page one and screaming, "Me, Me!"

You would think, with all these books about life's most important subject—you—that people would be more and more fulfilled, happy, satisfied, and successful. After all, we know how to be our own best friend, how to wake up in bed together, how to fight creatively, how to cook without salt, and yet, this heaping platter of self-help is served up in a never-ending banquet of print to a seemingly insatiable public starved for guidance. And with it all, the divorce rate keeps rising.

Rather than helping, "How To" books are inadvertently making the problems worse. Incredibly, no one has commented on how destructive these books with their communication "tricks" are. By suggesting self-growth and actualization, they promote selfishness and self-centeredness. Singles become so rigidly narcissistic they cannot possibly function as part of a team, and married people, swamped by self-awareness, wind up splitting. Not that splitting is always bad. It is just an inevitable and often forgotten consequence of these self-centered psychologies. Yes, divorce can aid some, but it should be kept in mind as a deliberate act, not a forgotten by-product. Popular psychology books, even those not self-oriented but for the specific purpose of helping people, married or unmarried, stay together, have failed to slow the divorce rate and even contributed to it. If a man and woman are ready to kill each other, advising them to "rope off their bed and have a pretend fight" may look good on the page but it is dangerous and evil in practice. These books fail because they invariably address themselves to the symptomatic treatment of problems without any attention given to the causes. The causes may be known and written about but never seem to be included in the cures. If you understand *why* you cannot get along, then a new trick to get along is not the answer. You must do something about the cause. Despite their printed promises, marital-help books cannot teach you a "nice" way to tell anyone creatively, aggressively that he or she is a lousy lover and a lousy mate. These books have hopelessly jammed the lines of communication. We believe, rather than opening them further, it is better to shut up.

"Shut up." Have you ever read a modern American book on marriage or psychology which tells its readers to be quiet? The advice is always talk out, feel out, or scream out your woes and they will go away. We're telling you to shut up. Not forever (though some things we'll discuss later are better left unsaid) but until you have carefully and thoughtfully reviewed your situation. Once you stop

tossing the beanbag of blame back and forth, you'll find it easy enough to communicate.

In this book, we are going to discuss the benefits of *not* breaking up, because we believe marriage is worth saving. There is warmth, dignity, encouragement, comfort, and fun in a good union. An old friend, a familiar shape, provides roots and continuity and should not be abandoned lightly. In the following chapters we'll describe the seven most serious reasons for splitting— Boredom, Leisure Time, Sex, Fights, Children, Money, and Careers. These can be danger areas, but if you look at them, it's obvious the same list could be used to describe the seven most valuable reasons for remaining together! We offer sensible potbelly-stove philosophy for a microwave-oven generation because it is the best way to warm a marriage. If your marriage has cooled, if there is a chill in your relationship, if you are touched or beset with problems, we will show you how *not* to succumb to them, how *not* to split up.

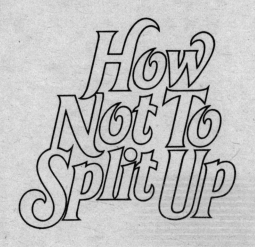

BOREDOM

BOREDOM IS UN-AMERICAN. As a nation we are afraid of it and we get into all kinds of trouble avoiding it. We cheat on spouses, change them, drink, gamble, spend too much money, start second careers, drive too fast, move West... anything to avoid the pain of monotony. Were Dante writing his *Purgatorio* today he would surely have to expand his list of seven deadly sins. What are lust, gluttony, avarice, sloth, anger, envy, or pride compared to the greatest sin of modern time, ennui? Being bored is deadly and being a bore is even deadlier. Americans just won't accept monotony as they did in past generations and perhaps still do in other parts of the world. From California to Massachusetts, tedium is the enemy, but we do not attack the foe. We dodge and try all manner of camouflage tricks to keep the doldrums away. Running from boredom has become institutionalized. It has names like "mid-life crisis," and a person is practically obliged to have one or at least *want* to change and start over.

"Tenure" is a powerful word in academia, but outside the universities it holds little fascination. There is no great universal chair or "professorship in Staying Power." Remaining with the same spouse or job is an oddity, and pressure is brought to bear on those who stick. We all feel these pressures. Whatever the situation—career, home, family—whenever we confess to a condition of longevity, we have to expect a put-down. It is rather amazing that this attitude exists in a country which until a few years ago rewarded people for long-term relationships, even "boring" ones. Loyal workers could expect engraved gold watches at the end of a long service; loyal wives and husbands rewarded each other on anniversaries. But we are no longer feted for staying in the same place, doing the same thing, or being with the same person. Instead, we are derided for not having the guts to get out.

It's a hit-and-run era and we frantically hide from dullness, repetition, and tediousness. As a result "fear" and "avoidance" of boredom have become more common than the state of boredom itself. We are confused and can no longer differentiate between boredom and daily life. They have become one and the same and nothing holds more promise than the magic word "evening"—that is the witching time when our fairy godperson is going to wave the magic activity wand and turn the commonplace into the scintillating. If that sounds farfetched, try calling friends at night and see how many you can find at home. Theater, dinner, discothèque, movie—it's always something to alter the pace of the (every) day. Although change and activity can certainly go a long way to relieve boredom, it is not always effective; this is especially true in marriage. If you are bored with each other and go out together, you are still stuck with one another at the end of the evening. You can't solve problems and ease bad feelings by running away from them. It is much more effective to stand still, drop the camouflage, face the situation, and solve it.

The Cultural Influences

In our country we have stockpiled a Fort Knox of cultural heritage, consisting of American traditions, legends, manners, and mores. To begin to understand marital boredom it is relevant to break into this subliminal social and intellectual vault and take a look at the history of our land to see how it has affected our manner of thinking.

MOVING ON

We are often unconscious of the ways in which the national myth of "moving on" to new opportunity has permeated our thinking. In fact and fiction this country was founded by forced or restless exploration, and much of the imagery connnected with these events influences us still. A kind of "Mayflower complex" tells us we must weigh anchor and sail away to bigger, better, and newer ports. Pilgrims, pioneers, astronauts, we are restless and suffer from national ants-in-the-pants. We move and climb and seek and move again. This is not a country of defeated, resigned people content with food and shelter and the quiet pleasures of family and community life. Such pursuits are taken for granted and seem boring. The immigrant climb from rags to riches, once a possibility for so many Americans, is now practically a bona fide pipe dream, yet we steadfastly cling to our domestic epic myths. We cannot forget that America was the land with "streets paved in gold." *You* can become wealthy and famous! And nowhere were those dreams more likely to come true than in the ultimate wagon-train stop, the "Dream Factory" itself, Hollywood.

GREAT EXPECTATIONS

Sip a soda in a drugstore. You are not mundanely quenching your thirst—you are about to become a *STAR!* Such fantasies are fun for a while. Eventually you must realize you are just sitting there waiting for something to happen, trying to recreate a fame-and-fortune fluke. The truth is, more movie stars are discovered under producers than over ice-cream sodas. And yet, the country, the movies, the William Morris Agency, your parents promised so much...the dream will not easily yield to the reality.

If that shopworn drugstore scenario can still hold such promise, imagine what marriage is supposed to do for you. "Sexual Fulfillment," "Companionship," "Sharing," "Growth"—all "star" in marriage. Well, they were supposed to; it was part of the 1930s and 1940s mystique of matrimony. Thanks to an endless parade of psychological articles and texts, everybody now knows you don't just fall into marital bliss; you have to communicate and work at it and it still may fail and it's better to live together unmarried for a long time, etc., etc., etc. When the myth of married bliss died, it was followed, as is all naïveté, by excessive cynicism. "Don't get married" became the cry and for "good" reasons: "Married people are bored and boring," "You need more than one sexual partner, maybe of more than one sex," "Women are exploited by their husbands," "Avoid the baby trap." These were the new tenets—yet the myth of happiness persisted: "the American Dream," "Life can by beautiful," "Everyday is a Hollywood premiere." The new way to achieve this dream is by living single or with some unmarried or by being sexually free. There has been no change in the national myth—we're still looking for the rainbow, but there is a detour in the Yellow Brick Road.

THE INTERNAL FRONTIER

The frontier of the West, followed by the two-car, split-level suburban frontier (augmented by the left-field illusion of Hollywood stardom), has been fully developed and replaced by the "internal" frontier. "Don't expand your business or wealth—expand your consciousness." "Become more aware of feelings." "Do something your forefathers could not—it is in the best spirit of America." "Your father may have made money, but he wasn't aware of his feelings the way you are." "Dad *worked* his way; you'll *feel* your way." This was the modern version of the pursuit of glory and the outstripping of the father, but it too is beginning to pass. The internal psychological frontier has been pretty thoroughly explored and is overrun with squatters—est, Esalen, etc. Further, it's hard to see how we could be *more* psychological. Part of the American myth, which made sense only in a new and growing and rich society, will have to be abandoned. The new generation will have to stop trying to surpass its parents and instead content itself with either being as good as or as different from but not necessarily bigger and better than the old. Statistics even show startling physical alteration. For the first time a generation will not be taller than the previous one. We can't expect to earn as much as Dad or to tower over him or in fact to have the same ideas about marriage. We must adjust, and when our expectations are modified, realistic forecasts about the pleasures, problems, and pains will replace the marital myths of happy-ever-after or happy-never-after. Once we are in the realistic groove and know what to expect, boredom in marriage can be better tolerated.

Realistic and Nonrealistic Boredom

Basically there are two kinds of boredom—realistic and nonrealistic. The former can be externally caused and the individual may have little if any control over relieving it. Working on an assembly line is the classic example, and this situation was explored to the fullest and funniest by Charlie Chaplin in *Modern Times* (1936). His assembly-line worker, perpetually fixing nuts to bolts in an ambidextral whirligig, finally goes berserk from the maddening sameness. He rushes into the street still wielding his dual monkey wrenches and tries to remove two strategically placed buttons from the jacket of a well-endowed matron. It is hilarious and horrifying. While Chaplin is *trapped* by monotony because he needs a job, certain kinds of people *volunteer* for boredom in order to feel safe. They could easily change the routine but they are afraid. Television's Archie Bunker *must* have eggs over, bacon, and toast lightly buttered *every* Sunday morning or else! Indeed a whole episode revolved around Archie's refusal to substitute bacon soufflé for his expected repast. Charlie is pushed into realistic boredom while Archie embraces it. Chaplin wants out from a terrible but necessary position, and his unconscious grants his wish. Archie Bunker really wants his Sunday breakfast constant and is comforted by the crisp sameness of bacon, toast, and fried eggs. Both are *realistic* adjustments to boredom, but there is another kind of boredom—*nonrealistic*—and for those in this category the odyssey never ends.

In nonrealistic boredom, *nothing* (conscious or unconscious) satisfies because the sufferer is unaware of what he wants and searches vainly for new restaurants, discothèques, vacation spots, people, sexual experiences, and, in general, goes to extraordinary lengths to relieve his boredom. He cannot satisfy the restless urge because he does not know at what it is aimed. This is termed "nonrealistic" because it is not justified on the basis of the facts either by its cause or its cure.

Both types of boredom can "touch" anyone, and how that person reacts to ennui's limp finger is very important.

THE LEVEL OF TOLERANCE

Whether it's realistic or nonrealistic, boredom is accompanied by painful feelings, and as with all feelings, boredom has its stoics and its complainers. Each of us have different levels of acceptance. One person can be depressed, say nothing, and carry on with a stiff upper lip, while another can't even get out of bed. One patient in the hospital moans loudly with pain, while another with the same disease and symptoms says little or nothing. Some adults, like infants, need to be distracted with an ever-shaking rattle. Others are more serene and do not need constant stimulation. *Increasing one's capacity to tolerate at least a reasonable amount of boredom is essential.* By no means does this imply resigned acceptance of tedium in all its manifestations. Minutes and perhaps hours of boredom ought to be tolerated, while months and years ought not and we must learn to combat boredom with the proper weapons. It is really a "duel." The complainers are unskilled and stab wildly and dumbly at boredom. *En garde!* They will not take this, they will not take that! Their flailing battle against monotony resolves itself in constant changes—job, location, spouse, anything. On the other hand, the stoics never bother to unsheathe their weapons and complacently allow boredom to apply the *coup de grâce.* Somewhere between these two extremes lies the answer. It's a happy medium requiring both the capacity to absorb a little punishment before crying "uncle," plus the ability to recognize the need for "change."

WHO'S TO BLAME?

The painful feeling accompanying boredom is a disagreeable one expressed through anger, restlessness, emptiness, apathy, or depression. Whenever any or all of these symptoms appear, we say we are "bored" and look for a reason. For example, a depressed man may attribute his "bad" feeling to his work and say, "My job is boring," or an angry woman suddenly declares the city she lives in "unbearably dull." Obviously, the bad feeling has to be the fault of a particular person, place, or thing. Married people don't have to go shopping around for a cause; they can simply use the nearest available reason—"my spouse." This reaction is a natural outgrowth of childhood and echoes the litany of adolescence: "I didn't do it, he did!" "It's not my fault, it's hers!" "Don't blame me!" However, at this point in maturity, it is far wiser to substitute a different childhood tune: "I'll show you mine if you show me yours." In other words *what* is wrong must be exposed, not *who* is wrong. The temptation to put the blame on someone or something else is almost irresistible, but you should try to avoid it.

ARE YOU BORED?

Deciding whether you are bored by your marriage is not so difficult once you understand what marital boredom is and become alert to it. We Americans are very skillful at hiding from feelings in general and boredom specifically, so the first thing to do is stop and think . . . not about your husband or your wife but about yourself. What, for instance, is your general level of tolerance for the unpleasant? Are you a complainer or a noncomplainer? What happens when you hit your crazy bone, stub your toe, get a headache? If your tolerance for pain is too low then you are liable to react the same way to a hangnail as you do to root-canal work. How about your tolerance for boredom? What happens when you see a dull movie or bump into a boring friend? Do you eat the same lunch every day? Your reactions can tip you off as to whether your tolerance for pain and boredom is too low. Paradoxically, tolerance can also be too high. Some people are so accepting of pain and boredom they don't even realize their lives are dull and dreary.

WHAT ABOUT YOUR MARRIAGE?

How *about* your marriage? Answer these few simple questions honestly: "Are you able to dine alone with your spouse or do you need a cast of characters either real (children) or televised (Walter Cronkite)?" "Would you be able to take a vacation together for a week or two, or must you arrange for family/friends to be along?" "Do you ever talk to each other about anything interesting or are you just verbal about bills and responsibilities?" If you cannot or do not do these things together, then you have a problem, either real or potential, and pretty soon you'll be blaming your marriage.

Marriage is a long-term, intimate relationship which causes buried conflicts and childlike needs to surface. The more unresolved childhood problems the adult has, the more likely he is to make unreasonable infantile demands on his spouse. Some people who are able to cope with tough business problems and settle world disputes in the office find themselves feeling needy around the hearth. They wish to be passive and taken care of rather than to make decisions. Even industrial and political tycoons who build and destroy companies and empires during the day use babytalk at home and call their wives "Mummy."

The plain fact is that many people expect too much from marriage. They are bored by their jobs and bored because of their own lack of resources and imagination to make life interesting, or they are bored because they do not know what they want out of life. No activity satisfies them, and so at the end of the day they present this huge gift-wrapped dissatisfaction to their spouse with the unconscious wish "unwrap it and make it better." When the spouse cannot properly play Mr. or Mrs. Fix-It, the partner becomes angry and disappointed and stops trying. He or she no longer carefully packs up all the cares and woes to bring home to Mama or Papa. When one partner stops trying soon the other stops trying too and then a marriage does in fact become boring.

• • •

Here are other questions: Do you look forward to meeting your spouse at the end of the day and sharing your thoughts and feelings? If not, did you ever and when did it change? If never, why did you marry in the first place? You can easily rate yourself on marital boredom by thinking about whether your spouse's ideas and company intrigue you, whether you find excuses to stay away from each other, whether you always need others around and whether you drink and eat too much when you're together. Another way to decide if you are unfairly blaming your marriage for your ennui is to think about your attitudes toward other aspects of life. Were you frequently bored before you met your mate and is this current "blah" simply more of the same? Are you often bored when *not* near your mate? (Be careful about this; people are too ready to blame spouses for faults within themselves.) If the answer is yes, then your problem is personal and not a fault of the marriage. Now, ask yourself what it would take to satisfy you. That's not so easy. "If only my wife were more interesting," moans the man on the couch. "What's 'interesting'?" asks the psychiatrist. "Oh I don't know," says the man. "I guess women aren't interesting. Come to think of it, hardly anything is interesting." If the personal is perplexed the marital can only be likewise.

The Marriage Syndromes

While boredom in a long marriage is inevitable and to be expected, if too much is accepted, it means each party has turned off from the other and settled for too little. Such marriages are usually comfortable and inevitably boring. If neither femme nor fella fatale appears on the scene, these relationships are not in imminent danger of actually splitting. Why? Because they are already split! Yes, the partners successfully avoid the pain and expense of divorce, but they get practically zero from their union and, not surprisingly, from life in general. They are "married splits." Each partner is plugged into the marriage, but one is AC, the other, DC. By supplying different currents to their union, they are not really together, and without questioning, they allow their marriage to move into married splitdom. One thing is certain—believing that marital boredom is inevitable increases its certainty, and by going along with it, you increase your chances of being married splits.

HOW DID IT HAPPEN?

You have now carefully reviewed your life and your marriage and by the process of elimination have concluded that you truly are a victim of marital boredom and that the cause comes from within the marriage itself. You are wearied by dullness, tedious repetition, and the unwelcome attentions of your spouse. The question is, how did it happen? You would never tolerate such predictability on your job or in the rest of your life, so how did you ever let it creep into your marriage? Most likely, you let it happen by succumbing to a leading cause of marital boredom: *clinging to rigid routine.* Now, why would you do that when you hate the humdrum? You don't cling to rigid routine elsewhere in your life and welcome change and variety. The answer is that you did it in your marriage because you were afraid to expose yourself, to make yourself vulnerable to your partner. Have you been guilty of maintaining status quo to avoid the risk of being hurt or engulfed or abandoned?

Maintain your cool and if your husband leaves you for a young chick, it won't hurt so much because he was "such a bore anyway." Maintain your cool and your wife gets you those two martinis between 6:00 and 7:30 each evening. It is expected, the duty will be performed, and neither of you has to face the potentially threatening subject of what you really want from the other and the possible hurt of not getting it. You want understanding, compassion, love; you settle for alcohol. Rigid routine limits exposure to pain. It anesthetizes you, but it also avoids your deeper needs and therefore leaves you bored and dissatisfied, especially with your marriage. You are not addressing what you really want but are lost in silly formality. In the case of the Martini Mates, the boredom and dissatisfaction lead to increases in the dose of the painkiller—more martinis. Advice to such couples to experiment is useless. Change frightens them and the best they could do is substitute an occasional manhattan.

THE BORE WAR

Couples get bored and build up elaborate defenses to combat the feeling. Some get drunk together every night. Unless they're "high," they cannot stand one another's company. They are "married splits," and Jim Beam and Jack Daniel are co-respondents. Other couples either go out all the time or make sure there's company for dinner. Lots of unhappy duos hide behind or around the children. In fact, this *Kinder* dependency is a leading cause of the empty-nest syndrome. When the children leave home, a couple may face each other alone for the first time in perhaps twenty-five years and they are shocked to discover how little they have in common. An overactive social and charitable life is another way to hide from marital boredom. There are people so busy running from luncheon to luncheon and meeting to meeting, they rarely step foot in their own living rooms. Working too much is no better. The man who stays in the office until ten at night may be avoiding marital boredom *and* pleasures; so is the wife who prefers him there. The "bore war" is a series of retreats on both sides.

PEACE AT ANY PRICE

It makes sense to ask couples to try and imagine what opening themselves to their partner might mean. Married people have some common fears about each other which may or may not be well founded. Do you, for instance, regard your husband as a bottomless pit of sexual drives? Would he want or do you fear he would want intercourse with its pre-and post-embellishments every day, while you either hate the whole business or wish to see him twice a month? Isn't it better to keep him liquored up? Do you see your wife as a demanding insatiable person, ready to swallow you up with clinging wishes? Would she order you about, causing you to resist? These could lead to fights and dramatic scenes. Rigid routine avoids this pain. "Drink and then you will forget." Boredom in such instances is a welcome compromise to open warfare. Even though both partners say they are bored and hate it, they in fact welcome the peace, however cold and dull, preferring it to the terror of open aggression.

You must begin to attack the rigid dullness born of terror in order to combat boredom. Once the fearful root is exposed, it's time to start pruning. If a lovely flowering tree grows in your yard and you want it to realize its full potential then you carefully tend it. Hacking off huge branches does not make a great tree. A snip here, a snip there, and soon the buds gain strength and fill out. If your "lovely" marriage is not flowering, then you must apply the same principles. Gradualism is never as upsetting as upheaval and is the basis of almost all behavior therapies. Anxiety is often based on a fearful and inaccurate appraisal of consequences of action, and people are surprised to find that their worst fears aren't realized. You may discover that your husband either never was or certainly is not now the "sex fiend" you anticipated. He does not pursue you with priapic persistence. If by some chance you were right and he wants intercourse in abundance, isn't it better to negotiate with him directly on that issue than sit and bore each other to death over cocktails? Negotiation is a skill essential to marriage. Without it, most marriages will either split or become empty and unsatisfying. One thing is certain, if your own attempts to resolve the problems of rigid routine repeatedly fail, you may need a third party to help. Married partners cannot continually *avoid* each other and must *open* themselves to each other.

The Forms of Regression

The most common cause of true marital boredom is *failure to try*. Fear of failing makes for lack of effort. The partners are not necessarily lazy, in fact, they may be quite active elsewhere in their lives—excellent and stimulating company *except* with each other. Obviously, if they are angry and resentful toward one another, they cannot talk freely and animatedly. Before anger, before aggression, lurks the common prior cause: regression. This happens when a person loses some of the development that his personality had already attained while reverting to a lower level of integration, adjustment, and expression. For example, Mr. Smith is a stuffy lawyer or responsible loan officer. All day long he makes pin-striped pronouncements. At night he returns home, tired of negotiating, controlling himself, being polite, making decisions. He wants to relax. The cliché is inevitable. He sits in front of the television and drinks his beer, loosing himself in video froth and Budweiser foam. He is unwilling to discipline the children or even to speak to his wife other than utter the perfunctory "Where's dinner? What's on tonight?" A working wife may respond in kind. Then neither mate wants to do anything. Fights take place about who should do which household chore, each complaining they have worked harder than the other.

These fights produce no champions; the winner is boredom.

THE MARITAL PLAYPEN

Regression often sets in the very first year of marriage, and if not checked, can lead directly to marital boredom. The phenomemon is noticed over and over again in clinical practice and can be called "regression of the first year of marriage." It happens especially in those marrying at an early age. And why not? They have recently completed adolescence, during which time separation from parents and families occurs. Generally this process is completed in the late teens or early twenties. A marriage at this time may take place before the process of separation from family has been either completed or firmly established. The marriage itself may be a way to dodge the pain involved in going out on one's own. Time and again, couples describe early marriage as a way to "spring loose" from undesired family situations. But these people really have not firmly established their independence. Their "grown-up" marriage is merely an opportunity to be helpless and get childhood needs fulfilled without paying the parental "piper." Immature couples are often unaware of what is going on and they experience personal and marital symptoms of regression. Young brides take to their beds and begin to think in terms of Excedrin rather than ecstasy. Young grooms become lackadaisical and put on weight. Soon they are both "depressed." Each may blame this on the partner or on vague reasons: "I married too young," "I feel badly about losing my freedom." They do not realize that they have regressed to a childlike level of expectation and the partner (mother/father substitute) is unable to fill their needs. Needless to say, these young people are not very interesting to one another. They expect to be cared for, waited on, and entertained as they were "at home." Prince and Princess are unwilling or unable to assume the mantles of King and Queen, and they begin to bore each other to death. Fortunately, couples usually get past this early setback. The wife drags herself out of bed and the husband takes off weight. Maybe she decides to take a job. Somehow they pull themselves together and out of the marital playpen. Others do not get over this stage and irreparably damage the marriage. They split. When this happens, they may at first feel much better because they are forced to be independent and care for themselves once again. If they go right into another intimate relationship, they may repeat the process of helplessness. These people need to establish their independence sufficiently or they'll always be looking for someone else to live their lives for them. They are too big for the crib and no one's going to rock them eternally. Couples caught up in this first-year regression need to treat one another as they did *prior* to marriage, taking the trouble to be sexy and interesting rather than passive, silent, and helpless. They need to treat each other as "grown-ups."

EGOCENTRISM:
THE ME EVERYONE SHOULD KNOW

Another variety of regression takes place in all marriages and indeed in all families. Except when it goes too far, it is not necessarily pathological or bad. It is, after all, a competitive hard world out there and it's nice to come home to one's nest and let down one's guard. There's a bit of that "pin-striped Mr. Smith" in all of us. Outside we are rewarded for our politeness and charm, inside we want to drop the façade and be accepted, warts and all. We take off our business suits and want also to remove the armor of our outside persona. There's a reason why home has been termed a "haven" and a "castle"; it's the one place where we can be ourselves. The tone is established in childhood. Generally speaking, children rarely behave as well at home as they do elsewhere. How many mothers have said, "I wish your teacher and your friends could see you as you really are!" The implication: the child, mean and rotten at heart (at home), only pretends to be nice with others. Little girls and boys neatly pick up after themselves and make the beds when staying at a friend's, but they would never think to do so at home without a fight or a reminder. We relive such family behavior patterns with our spouses. "I'm *home*, I'm *me!*" and we don't try to please. It is very rare for husbands and wives to ask themselves whether they take the trouble to be interesting to the spouse. The feeling is "I'm tired from the day and I shouldn't have to *try* to be anything but myself at home. When Mummy wanted me to do something she had to dig it out of me, and I'm not volunteering now!" Even those who did toe the mark in childhood want to stop doing so after marriage and claim that their upbringing was "uptight." They refuse to make "hospital corners" in their marriage and want to hang loose. Relaxation rules the roost. Thoughts of being interesting to or interested in the spouse fly out the window, and along with those thoughts often goes common courtesy. People stop talking to one another because the spouse pays no attention to the one speaking. He or she watches television, continues reading the newspaper, interrupts, looks out the window, or walks away. The husband stops talking about his business. Why? Not only does his wife fail to respond with any intellectual grunts, she is openly bored. The wife stops talking about her job or their kids because he hides behind the headlines. Nothing is said. Result? Boredom.

The solution is relatively simple. Husband and wife should treat each other as they would an eminent stranger! Think about that for a while. Overcome the childish feeling of "I don't have to try at home." It will make life a lot more pleasant if you take the trouble to interest one another. And it is not merely a question of conversation. You would not dine in the same place, wear the same clothes, or be otherwise dull and repetitive with someone you were trying to impress or stimulate, so why do it with your wife or husband? It is true that parents and children take each other for granted as do husband and wife, and it is also true there is plenty of family trouble in America. Not a little of this attitude is caused by the "indifferent" treatment we heap on those we "love."

Really, if you don't have the stuff to take the trouble you would with a man or a woman you were trying to interest and apply it to your dealings with wife or husband, then be prepared to be bored.

The "home-is-my-haven" regression can cause a retreat to a very self-centered, narcissistic form of behavior, accompanied by a failure to sense what the spouse wants and needs. Both partners are bored. Something is wrong and the husband decides to take action. Why not do something thoughtful? Bring home flowers. Advice columnists must be in cahoots with the Society of American Florists since all of them suggest the husband bring home a bouquet from time to time. That's fine. But supposing your wife craves a new blouse or needs a new toaster? Mightn't she resent the fact you spent money on flowers she didn't really want? The point is that you cannot just take action; you have to pay attention to your spouse to know *what* action to take. If you are presumptuous about the solution, you cannot improve the situation. It is very self-centered to think you know the answer without asking the question.

In our "me-me" generation, a lot of people don't *regress* to self-centeredness—they never passed it by in their development. It is impossible for them to sink "back" into something they've been wallowing in since childhood. Excessive narcissism makes successful marriage virtually impossible because of the person's inability to sense the needs of anyone else and his or her unrelenting focus on taking. The excessively egotistical partner never realizes that marriage is a barter system, in which taking must be followed by giving. Those who don't know or don't act on this knowledge, end up alone. If you do know (or if you're just learning), it's half the battle and you can change by making an effort.

LET'S PRETEND

If you've been told repeatedly by your spouse, close friends, and family members that you don't think enough of others and if you've decided to do something about it, you should begin by taking the trouble to think about your spouse and *pretend* to be concerned. Before you get mad and think this odd advice (first, to "shut up" and now to "sham") consider this: any new behavior initially feels strange. At a certain point people stubbornly, defiantly, or matter-of-factly feel "I'm me, there's nothing I can do about it so I must be accepted for what I am." Don't step into this ego trap. You must be willing to change, but it isn't easy to assume a new role. Like a great actor preparing for a part, you have to take certain steps. Eleanora Duse, the famous tragedienne, went out into the streets of Italy observing people from all walks of life to see how they behaved, how they acted and reacted. She applied what she learned to her theatrical interpretations and this insight and planning helped make her the foremost actress of her day. There was depth in her portrayals, and it brought her characters to life. That was on stage, but in real life the same principles apply. Whenever you try to be different you must at first feel false. Any new situation is awkward. A third-year medical student starting on the wards is called "Doctor" and looks around wildly for someone else. He will be, in time, quite comfortable in the role of physician, but the newness makes him feel like a fraud. A selfish person attempts generosity and the change from Silas Marner to Santa Claus is clumsy. It is truly more difficult to give than receive. Be as persistent as Duse. The initial steps will be crude—the beginning is made in pretense but the result can be honest, effective change. You must be willing to feel uncomfortable and insincere at first. However, if you get nothing back, you will understandably lose interest. If your spouse says, "I don't trust you, you're not being sincere, a leopard doesn't change his spots," try to counter with patience. "Yes, my efforts are awkward but don't concentrate on my style; look at the *intent*." It is okay to take criticism and anger for a little while but feel free to tell your mate to knock it off, if he or she doesn't begin to respond positively. After all, you are trying and so must your partner.

Solutions

Once rigid routine, excessive regression, and self-centeredness have been recognized, there are some practical things couples can do to make marriage more interesting. Remember, there are *two* of you—only saints are single—and two people must interact. Response and invention are as important as initial action. Since repetition and predictability are at the center of boredom, variety is an obvious way to cope with this problem. Think of marriage as a great *bel canto* aria. Apply the techniques of embellishment to the most basic routines and the results could delight you.

BOARD VERSUS BED

If marriages could be "excavated," the dining room would definitely be unearthed as a prime site of boredom. A good marriage must be fed. We work to make money for food and shelter, and if our food and shelter are dreary, well, what the hell are we working for? Mealtimes are activities which most married couples share (breakfast and dinner, if not lunch). There are, in fact, far more cases of couples who don't have sex together than those who don't have dinner together. Certainly, more time is devoted to the preparation, execution, and cleanup of meals than to intercourse. Lack of co-operation and enjoyment at the dinner table can be every bit as big a problem as any dilemma of the bedroom. There are many times when Julia Child and James Beard can be of more assistance to your marriage than William Masters and Virginia Johnson. Yet this "undramatic" activity is not the subject of much psychiatric research or popular writing. Recently the relationship between good food and good sex was established in an article by a psychiatrist, obstetrician, psychologist, and nutritionist in the *Archives of General Psychiatry*. The study was made to test the Freudian theory that oral people fixate on food, while genital people are mature and sexual. Freud's theory hypothesized that people who loved food would be less likely to love sex. The new study disclosed the opposite! Those who love food, love sex. It does make sense—a zest in one area is accompanied by a vitality in another. Cookbooks are enormously successful best sellers, but many superb meals are ruined by angry silence, television, or newsprint. Since the dinner table is a potentially ripe site for boredom, you must work together to change the scene. Become interested in food; try new dishes. Wives have powerful allies. Every weekly and monthly magazine devotes pages and pages to recipes. *Good Housekeeping, Redbook, Cosmopolitan, Family Circle, McCall's,* and *Ladies' Home Journal* instinctively knew what the *Archives of General Psychiatry* had to discover. You have the resources so experiment. If you fail, why, forget it and try again. Patience is as essential as parsley at the table, especially for the newlywed wife. All those jokes about burnt toast didn't spring out of nowhere. Remember, too, your whole life and reputation don't depend on your being perfect all the time. As a matter of fact, expect to fail sometimes and it will give you the resiliency to hang in. In modern marriages, men are cooking more often. They may contribute a "specialty" to everyday meals. Encourage your husband, and gastronomic adventures can become another shared pleasure.

Other things about dining can be varied, including the time, the room, and the dress. Any woman who appears at the table crowned with plastic curlers or covered by a gunny-sack housedress deserves to be boiled in her own pudding. Appetite is connected to sight, and the wrong apparition can spoil the finest feast. Americans have moved away from the formal and no longer really "dress" for dinner, but you should at least "tidy up" and present yourself at your best.

Arrange occasionally to have a guest, either with your spouse's consent or as a nice surprise. Ask someone bright or interesting of just plain attractive and don't invite anyone whose company is not desirable to both. You are trying to add spice to the table, not compound the boredom. And if your spouse turns up at the door with a surprise guest, you needn't fall apart—just put out another setting. Don't confine your entertaining to weekends. A dinner guest doesn't have to stay late and you don't have to go to unnecessary lengths to please—just to imaginative ones. It *is* difficult for two people to entertain each other year in and year out and an occasional outsider makes it easier. Never become too dependent on the company of others, though; that's one of the boredom traps. Simply balance your guests as you do your diet.

BUILDING YOUR NEST
AND OTHER JOINT ENDEAVORS

It is wise to literally "build your nest" together. Men are missing out if they don't participate to some degree in furnishing and decorating the home. Sometimes you won't agree and you may even fight over a "coffee table," but it's worth it. Looking in antique shops or going to auctions and showrooms can be fun and it is a shared activity.

Once it is decorated, change your home around. The Japanese have recognized the importance of change for centuries. In their homes, scrolls, pictures, vases, and other *objets d'art* are rotated, sometimes with the seasons. It is too predictable to keep the same thing in the same place, and you do not have to invest in new furnishings—just switch around what you have. Don't surround yourself with "still lifes." Change.

Although couples cannot possibly share all interests, they must enjoy some as a duo. Variety will fall flat on its face if the couple isn't pulling together. Try simple pleasures like reading to each other. This is a wonderful family custom and does not mean you must take down the Bible and plow through Deuteronomy every day. You can easily substitute best sellers.

Involve your partner in a unique aspect of your life such as shopping for clothes. Again, you don't need an escort for every shopping foray, but once in a while it's exciting to parade before your partner in a new get-up. Also, you can avoid money squabbles later if the price tag is agreed upon ahead of time.

Adding to each other's knowledge and experience is a great opportunity for married people. Baseball and football usually have bad connotations for the distaff side, but why not try to watch a little of the sports that mean so much to your spouse? Effort must be met with response. If a wife joins in the activity, then the husband must not abuse the situation. The ancient Greeks did not have televised sports events to contend with, but they wisely argued, "Nothing in excess." This does not mean you must turn the set off in the last moments of a seventh-game tie in the World Series or go and have a cup of tea just as O. J. Simpson is racing for record-breaking yardage, but it does mean you could relent a bit and not spend the entire afternoon impacted in the TV tube. Try and get your spouse interested in your activity. If you take the time, you may wind up with a fan instead of a disgruntled mate.

CREATING THE OCCASION

A good marriage should be a series of great and small occasions made possible by each partner. Even if you are a housebound mother, there is no reason why you cannot have a "story" for your husband when he comes home. Cultivate an eye for detail and take the trouble to share what you've seen. Children provide an excellent source of material. They are fascinating in their ideas and in the ways their minds unfold. Jean Piaget, the Swiss child psychologist, developed most of his significant theories by watching the development of his *own* children. You don't have to give a blow-by-blow description of the emergence of each tooth, but you can apply the techniques of embellishment to make the tales of "Johnny and Sue" exciting.

In or out of marriage, all days are important, but it is the "occasion" that stands out and occasions must be created. Birthdays are obvious points of departure; they can be times of great pleasure and not dreary reminders of age. Whether you are on the giving or receiving end, you must cultivate a second naïveté and be willing to be led into "childlike" wonder. Which means, for example, even if you *know* there's a surprise party waiting for you at home, you enjoy it to the fullest. The most charming, least bored people have the capacity to be excited by something. If you do not have this quality, then acquire it just as you would a new "behavior." Pretend at first and soon it will come naturally. When you achieve it in genuine fashion, you will enjoy your life so much more and find that others are genuinely drawn to you. Creating an occasion takes you away from your day-to-day life and gives you something to look forward to. In truth, the best way not to have a boring marriage is not to be a boring person. Be prepared to entertain *yourself* as well as others. If you look less to your spouse to stimulate you, there will be less pressure on the *marriage* to provide interest and it will seem less tedious to be two.

THE JOY OF BOREDOM

Are there joys in boredom? Yes. Dull can lull. There is security in knowing certain things will be unchanging. Americans have a love-hate relationship with sameness. We champion change, yet we are always impressed by tradition. For instance, we like our Sunday Dinner. It's a family institution you can rely on. It doesn't always have to be roast chicken and apple pie, but it will be Sunday together around the table. It's a secure feeling and in sameness there is trust.

In the long-term relationship called marriage, behavior

has to become *somewhat* predictable. Your partner is a certain kind of person and you have a pretty good idea how that person will react. That's when smart partners start delivering the "change-up." But even if every ploy against boredom is used, it will come, and remember that in manageable doses it comes replete with security and trust and comfort. Comfort doesn't always mean fat and stupid. Comfort allows you time to save and store energy that would be otherwise squandered for nothing. This energy can be applied to creative efforts.

Take a little comfort together, but keep yourself interesting, too, and you have a better chance to make your marriage the same. James Russell Lowell wisely wrote in *A Moosehead Journal*, "There is no bore we dread being left alone with so much as our own minds."

LEISURE TIME

ALMOST EVERYTHING IN our past fails to prepare us for our leisure, particularly our education. Vocational and professional schools and colleges train us to be plumbers, electricians, pilots, computer programmers, doctors, lawyers, and auto mechanics but not how to use our "free" time. Furthermore, although they ought to, many of the courses we take usually don't help in adult life. We forget French, don't read Shakespeare, never think about mathematics, don't care about the causes of the Civil War, the theory of electricity, or the product of mixing sodium chloride and sulfuric acid. Have you read anything by Thoureau since you left high school or by Plato since you left college? Liberal arts courses may connect with the few, giving them a lifelong interest in reading history or viewing works of art, but for the overwhelming majority of the "liberally" educated, little or no continuing value carries over into adulthood. In most institutions, especially Ivy League ones, it's hard to get credit for learning how to do things you might enjoy later in life like playing the violin. When you think of it, even school sports don't make much future sense. The emphasis is often on baseball, football, soccer—games requiring large groups of players, groups you almost never find or take the trouble to assemble when you are older. Almost everything is group-oriented and that's probably why thirty- and forty-year-olds embrace "singular" sports like tennis, skiing, squash, golf, horseback riding, and bicycling with such wild enthusiasm.

In our schools, prestige and status, labor's attendants, are also taught and encouraged directly or subtly. Professors, long on bibliographies and short on time, inspire the young. Constantly traveling, consulting with business and governments, these busy, fragmented men and women are no longer a familiar part of campus life. The student doesn't really know his professors; instead, he admires their achievements. The better schools have the busier professors, and their lack of availability is no secret. They are shining examples of the virtue of "all work and no play." No wonder their pupils graduate unprepared for leisure.

The Work Ethic

We have no respect for leisure time because we have been trained and educated by those with very little. Work is everything, almost a religion, and we live by the "Protestant work ethic." When we have time on our hands, we are uneasy—life is empty, devoid of meaning. Once we hopelessly yearned for *rest* from unremitting toil; now we worry about the painful void of free, empty, monotonous time.

The work ethic dictates the pattern of our lives both on and off the job. Time becomes so valuable that its use must be carefully rationed in an effort not to waste it. Hurry up, please, there's no time. On vacation we jet to Europe rather than float. We have traded the gracious shipboard life—romances on the leeward side, friendship around the dinner table, strolls on the promenade deck—for quick, jammed trips in winged sardine cans. Hurry up, please, there's no time. Who bothers to lovingly create a memorable meal? We thaw and microwave and are Cuisinarted to death. We are Birdseye gourmets. Hurry up, please, there's no time. A fifty-five-mile-an-hour speed limit seems like standing still. Such a bother when we have to race home Saturday night because we have so much to do on Sunday. Hurry up, please, there's no time! And don't overlook the ultimate in our measured leisure—women practically created a national movement to lengthen the moments devoted to foreplay! Please don't hurry up, take time!

THE LURE OF THE RAT RACE

The ambition to earn more, to advance one's fame and position, to produce, to use time wisely—all influence our every activity. We don't read novels so much as books that help us earn more to get ahead. We go to parties to make contacts, not for a "good time." Business lunches are tax-free, profit-motivated; if we retire or change companies, our old associates no longer want to see us—why bother?—there's no further business purpose. We give cocktail parties for a cause, not for fun. We are scared to death of "enjoying ourselves" to no purpose and unconsciously scheme and work under the guise of leisure in order to square social activities with our consciences before we can have a good time. "Let's get together for a drink" is as archaic a request as "Let's get together for a chariot race." Instead, we say, "Let's get together and talk about the accounts or building the new opera house or starting a planned *parenthood* clinic." These utilitarian motives often veil the thinly disguised wish to just pass the time, but people find it hard to admit they crave companionship so they must pretend to be working at some serious purpose. And what happens when we are in our "haven," our "castle," the one place where we are licensed to "let go"? We are not at home to enjoy the company of our spouse and children but to get to "work"—to fix the leaky roof or repair Junior's bicycle. Many researchers believe this unrelenting rush has increased the heart attack rate in men, and in women too. Yes indeed, the purpose of life is work, and except for a few heretics here and there, almost all of us are afraid of true leisure.

What Is Leisure?

There are many ways to define leisure time. If you call it those hours free of work for pay, then struggling up a rickety ladder with a mouthful of nails to fix your roof is a leisure-time activity. Few of us would want to consider this chore as a leisure-time activity because it's dangerous, hard, physical labor. Is leisure, then, time completely free of commitments—that is, contemplative time? If so, how does spending Sunday with the kids fit into this definition? Surely we have a commitment to them as we do to spouses, in-laws, friends—even to the grand old Sunday tradition of washing the family car. But most of us are manacled figuratively by this narrow definition. We consider leisure to be time to think, sleep, read the newspaper, and watch television. Time completely devoid of commitments. The concept of leisure, however, must include an idea that we are using hours which we have control over. For our purposes, the best definition of leisure is "discretionary time."

THE REWARDS: MONEY

The executives and the professionals make more and more money but they work longer and longer hours.

Buying a thirty-foot sailboat makes the hours spent
sailing over the bounding main very expensive and means
fewer hours to do it. And a vacation home in a perfect
setting with a fabulous view can be visited and relaxed in
for fewer and fewer hours. The price of free time, time to
enjoy the fruits of labor, has gone up and up.

Aristotle believed the "goal of war is peace; of business,
leisure," yet the more some of us desire leisure, the less we
are able to take it—it costs too much! The high-wage
earners are on a work versus leisure treadmill, and
because they devote more and more hours to work, they
have not been sharing in the over-all growth of leisure
time.

THE REWARDS: SOCIAL STATUS

Unlike blue-collar workers, many professionals and
highly educated people derive rich satisfaction from their
labors because they can achieve professional and
financial success and enjoy high social status. Furthermore, the demand for their time has risen during the last
decade.

Although there is some blue blood coursing through
the proper veins in America, social status as such is
derived primarily from one's work. Henry Kissinger,
Frank Sinatra, Muhammad Ali, and Jonas Salk would
not have made the social register but are now welcome
almost everywhere. The "rewards" of work for the
educated, professional, or executive are indeed great.

THE POWER MAZE

Kissingers, Sinatras, Alis, and Salks are perhaps rare, but
the activity which makes them supersuccessful is not.
They worked for their fame and got it in extraordinary
doses, but there are also ordinary people desirous of
moderate success and they have to work just as hard as the
superachievers. The assistant vice president of a large

department store wants to rise up the ranks, get more money and power, and be recognized as a winner. For this he is willing to travel, be available to the boss at odd hours, accept transfers with a smile, work nights, and give up most, maybe all, of his leisure time. There is no other way. The young associate in a law firm will similarly get to his office at 8:00 or 8:30 A.M., take an hour or so for lunch and dinner, and work through until ten or even midnight. He will push, push, push, in hopes of becoming a six-figure-salaried senior partner or perhaps a supreme court judge. These men enter the maze without thinking, and before they turn the first corner they've lost their leisure.

AMBITION ISN'T EVERYTHING

Like the enterprising vice president and the aspiring lawyer, people get caught up in what they do, in their ambition. There is no choice between work and leisure. We must toil because it is necessary for self-esteem, success, and the feeling of well-being. It is a natural outgrowth of our upbringing and education. Having competed to get into the best college with the busy unavailable professors, encouraged by busy unavailable, ambitious parents, we rush into the rat race. It is an automatic response, almost an involuntary one, and there are no alternatives. Because the use of discretionary time is not taught, decisions regarding it are made emotionally, not rationally. The "drop-out" reacting to his absent, work-oriented father and his lonely, depressed mother decides to take menial part-time jobs and live at bare subsistence level so he won't be a slave to the rat race. The "highly motivated" buys the system and overworks the way his father did. Going hog-wild in either direction is not the answer.

THE SPURS OF FAME AND FORTUNE

Driven men cannot help but view the family as just another demand on their time, not a pleasure. Actually, those primarily desiring money are better off than the status seekers. Some believe you can never have enough money or as the slender savant Wallis Simpson, the Duchess of Windsor, partly put it, "You can never be too rich..." We dislike arguing with the Duchess, but she may not really have the answer: you *can* be rich enough. Setting one's sights for something *large* rather than something totally unreasonable in the way of a standard of living or salary is realistic. The game of reputation however, is hopeless—you're only as good as your last merger, movie, book, or play. Whatever you want, knowing *it* and going after *it* intelligently is essential.

Setting Life Goals

A bright law student in psychotherapy desired the good things in life, but he was also interested in high-quality leisure time. He decided strong marks in the Harvard Law School would allow him to get into one of the seventy "best" New York firms. Because he was brilliant even by Harvard's standards, he knew if he studied all the time he could get into the top one or two firms. This would bring him no more money than lesser firms, possibly not as much, since in the top few firms only a small percentage of beginning associates are asked to stay on as senior partners to draw those six-figure paychecks. The prestige of working for one, however, is great and among other things, our bright young lawyer could get to be a trustee of important organizations. It was a very tempting career to dangle before an ambitious young man, but this fellow decided the risk of not becoming a partner was not worth the possibility of dazzling social prestige. In the meantime, he could have a better time in law school, enjoying luncheon with friends, getting out in the evening, playing squash—in short, he could have some leisure. The hours and stress less, a future salary about the same, *his* choice was clear. He decided to ease up and opt for one of the less pressured firms.

In seeking life goals, priorities must be established at the beginning. The man who sets his sights reasonably is undoubtedly better marriage material than the "over-achiever." The woman married to the other kind, the one in the best firm, the budding Oliver Wendell Holmes, Jr., or the future Lyman or Joseph Bloomingdale, is probably upset right now. She might ask herself why she married him. Yes, she may say "It was love" or "He was different then," but she might be overlooking the fact that she wants a winner, a man who is important, rich, and celebrated. If that's what she wants, then she must be prepared to be alone a lot while her husband is out there achieving, *and* she'd better be ready to bring up children pretty much on her own. When she feels most lonely and neglected she should stop and ask herself if she too is ambitious and wants people to look up to her. If she's not willing to renounce all those red-carpeted obeisances that her husband's position dictates, then she should try to be less angry at the price she must pay. Great fame and togetherness aren't usually traveling companions, and ambivalent feelings about which is more important must be straightened out *before* marriage. A woman should be certain of her own needs and find a person who fits into the pattern of her life, not someone who will disrupt the balance.

THE DUO RAT RACE

Wives who live with work-oriented, ambitious men are lonely women. Young women of today, savvy about this, still seek ambitious men, but instead of staying home, join them in the race, dropping domesticity for the office and entering their own seventy-hour-a-week marathon. In certain cases, no matter how hard the husband works, the wife works harder; no matter how prestigious his career, hers is greater. "Anything you can do, I can do better" runs amok as husband and wife skid around the career maze. As a result of this duo rat race a new kind of divorce has emerged. The *man*, jealous of the woman's greater success, feels neglected by *her*.

Marriage between two seventy-hour-a-week workers does not work out very well, especially when there are children. These couples just don't have enough time together, leisure or otherwise. Ironically, such unions are often touted as "perfect" because these couples are clever enough to display a marvelous facsimile of wedlock by touching base here and there—but they are often "married splits" and use each other as decorative ornaments rather than helpmeets.

In ever-increasing numbers, women, the last possessors of leisure time, are trading it in for the independence and purchasing power that money gives them and the recognition and status that work gives them. "Poor" women have always labored—as domestics, laundresses, waitresses, seamstresses—but the women's movement of today emphasizes the rewarding work available to the educated. By working, these women might ideally liberate their long-hours men. However, the trend is not to share the burden but to join the competition.

Everyone in the work rat race is deserting the good ship *Leisure* and it is in danger of sailing out of sight permanently. That would be regrettable, for, as Kenneth Clark has pointed out, civilization is a product of leisure. When time is plentiful, there is the opportunity to make something beautiful, not just functional, and time to reflect.

Yes, modern men and women in their devotion to work have neglected leisure because the money they produce buys power and a feeling of self-worth. Ah, but the ghost of Leisure Past comes to haunt them and the question inevitably arises, "Maybe I've given up too much?" Too late, sometimes, the powers-that-be look back longingly at the good-times-that-were.

LEISURE CONSCIOUSNESS

Because people make many small, automatic decisions which ultimately lead to corporate enslavement, lack of leisure time, and destroyed marriages, it is necessary (as it was for that Harvard law student) to become conscious from the beginning of what is at stake. If the assessment is made early enough, then people will be better able to control how they divide their time between work and leisure. Once they figure it out, they can realistically and logically plan for the future. Increasing respect for leisure is a vital part of the master scheme. All work and no play not only makes Jack a dull boy—it also makes him a lousy mate, and the same is true for his wife.

I LOVE LEISURE

To take its rightful place in the life-picture, leisure has to compete better with work. Self-esteem has to come from good family life, friendship, sex, shared activities—in other words, leisure rewards should be as meaningful as work ones. The word "leisure" itself must have new connotations, not sinful or wasteful but necessary and important. Strangely enough, there is in our past a measure of precedence for the tolerant regard of leisure. At the same time we regard it with a jaundiced eye, we also look back to a slower moving age when it was possible to indulge in unhurried activities. We adore TV shows like "Happy Days" and "Laverne and Shirley" and movies like *Paper Moon, The Sting* and *American Graffiti* because they reweave the gossamer fabric of lost leisurely times. And yet we do everything in our power to prevent present-day youth from living in this way! The young come equipped with an understanding of leisure, but early on they're trained, nay, *coerced* out of their adolescent habits of "wasting" time.

Making Leisure Work for
Your Marriage

Leisure has to be treated well, actively, and creatively by married couples, and since there are, at this writing, no "leisure therapy clinics," couples must work with leisure on their own. It has to be handled carefully and intelligently or else you'll be faced with the old bugaboo boredom. Practice using leisure time yourself and then move into it as a couple. Remember, duo bores are solo bores first, and if you don't know how to use leisure singly, you'll have difficulty sharing it. When you deal skillfully with discretionary time and are satisfied, you'll demand less from your spouse.

RATING LEISURE TIME IN MARRIAGE

In *Diseases of the Nervous System* (January 1973), a practical journal on psychiatry and neurology, Chad Gordon, Charles M. Gaitz, and Judith Scott studied and reported on the leisure habits of 1,441 persons. They rated leisure activities from "very low" to "very high," according to the intensity of expressive involvement (cognitive, emotional, and physical). "Very low" included solitude, quiet resting, and sleeping. "Medium low" covered passive entertainment, for example, mass-media usage, reading, hobbies, games, toys of most kinds, socializing, entertaining, and spectator sports. "Medium" involvement occurred in serious reading, disciplined learning, studying a musical instrument, attendance at cultural events (art galleries, museums), organization participation (clubs, interest groups), sightseeing, and travel. "Medium high" activities embraced creative endeavors (artistic, literary, and musical) and serious discussion. "Very high" involvement occurred in sexual activity, ecstatic religious experience, aggression (either physical fighting or verbal argument), highly competitive games and sports, vigorous physical exercise, and dancing. In their study the researchers found the "active, social and external forms of activity rather than the passive, individual and homebound forms are predictive of psychological well-being." Their research supported the "old folk wisdom that active life-styles tend to produce more pleasure and reduce the loneliness, depression and anxiety of isolation." The best leisure is active and purposeful not "empty." Sometimes, to keep it from being "empty," we make the mistake of working too much.

Overworking is not the way to avoid leisure problems. Those hours of labor add up, leaving leisure a time of collapse or boredom. While it is comforting to "collapse" once in a while, it is a luxury, not a necessity. Don't use work as an excuse to flop down all the time or your marriage will start to sag, too. Sitting around, relaxing, drinking, and watching television while saying and accomplishing nothing will not keep you happy and stimulated for very long. You cannot and should not depend upon Johnny Carson, Mike Douglas and Merv Griffin to while away your hours and keep you occupied; that is not leisure, that is laziness. Learning to deal with leisure makes it something to look forward to rather than fear and anesthetize yourself against.

LACK OF LEISURE

Scarcity of leisure time has profound effects on such diverse areas as loyalty, affection, sex, and marriage. In particular, the middle-aged man in rootless, restless America often has no real and deep friendships—there is no time to establish new ones or even continue old ones.

Friendship suffers as does marital life, so much so that a most unorthodox organization reflecting this dilemma has recently surfaced. We've all heard of Alcoholics Anonymous, Weight Watchers, and the like, but did you know of Mistresses Anonymous? These women have banded together not to dry out or shed pounds but to share problems which revolve around their married lovers. The president of M.A. reported that, contrary to popular belief, errant husbands are more interested in sharing *mental* rather than *physical* intimacies! These men want to divulge secrets about their business and personal lives, to open up and "let it all hang out." In our times, *social* intercourse is harder to come by and more prized than *sexual* intercourse. The extent can be measured by the large number of wandering males looking for a good friend not a "good lay." In order to stay "off the streets," these lonely men will have to find solace and friendship at home. One way to do this is through the intelligent use of leisure hours, no matter how limited the time.

MAKING TIME FOR GOOD LEISURE

Several years ago, a *Time* magazine reporter followed a married couple for a week and discovered that they spoke to each other in that time for a grand total of twenty-nine minutes. Such a union is a sterile business relationship, to be endured not relished. You can't cram a week's worth of living into a skimpy half hour of dialogue. It takes time to have a workable marriage in which there are advantages and satisfactions for each partner. Then, there can be genuine pleasure in one another's company, absence of loneliness, affection, sexual attraction, contentment, and rapport arising out of shared activity.

A couple in therapy confessed to the therapist that once the dinner dishes were cleared and the kids put to bed, the "grass" came out and the two of them spent the remainder of the evening on Cloud Nine with the TV going full blast. Occasionally there was some fumbling

sex, but generally they were zonked. The therapist
pointed out that this was not quite the ideal way to spend
leisure hours together and suggested some substitutions.
These two are now trying to wean themselves from
Acapulco Gold and the "Late Show" by reading books
and talking to each other. Although they are not out of
the woods yet, they're at least trying to share a *higher* level
of leisure involvement. This is very important because a
marriage without good leisure time becomes a commer-
cial arrangement which doesn't meet the emotional needs
of the people involved.

SAVE ENERGY: ENJOY LEISURE

Lack of leisure time is a major marital problem and
running close second is *what to do with what you got!*
Problem two can be well met if you keep in mind that you
must *save enough energy for leisure*. The collapse
approach doesn't work. If the husband is exhausted from
overwork, propped up in front of the TV, drink in hand,
or snoozing on the sofa, leisure simply becomes a "pit
stop" in the work race. Your job provides you with
money, a sense of useful accomplishment, professional
success, and social status, and leisure cannot hope to
compete with the good feelings derived from work.
Admittedly, it's hard to admire yourself or get others to
look up to you because of how beautifully you sleep, how
gracefully you relax in your own backyard, how earnestly
you watch television, and how eagerly you drink whiskey.
A *higher* level of leisure-time activity is required to derive
those good feelings of approval, plus the admiration of
others, so there's got to be a change. Surely it's possible to
alter and practice a form of leisure activity other than
total passivity. Not only is it a waste of intelligence to
behave like a sand-logged clam, there are repercussions
all over the place, for instance, regarding sex.

SEX AND LEISURE TIME

Leisure is the forgotten subject in modern upbringing, taught neither in home nor in school, but arguments over whether sex should be taught in home or at school are constantly raging. Isn't it ridiculous to pay no attention to a subject which causes far more misery and conflict? Chances are if leisure were handled well and creatively, sex, a basically enjoyable act when performed without conflict and anger, would be much more pleasurable.

Dr. John F. Cuber, sociologist at Ohio State University, estimates that only about one of five upper-middle-class couples has an active and satisfying sex life. The husband is too tired and overworked, the wife is too lonely and depressed or tired and overworked too. The pressures and obstacles of their busy lives hit them hardest below the belt. One out of five can handle it; the remaining four couples plead exhaustion. Their pressured lives prevent them from fully enjoying sex, and don't forget, sex takes place during leisure time. You can see how the work ethic not only scorns the idle but leaves little time for sexual activity!

The Constructive Use of Leisure

A constructive way to handle leisure is to assess your own values. If discretionary time is used in accordance with your principles, then the onus of sin is lifted. You will be at ease with leisure and your family life will improve. Change your feeling from one of immoral waste to the intelligent use of time, over which you have control, and get in shape for it mentally and physically. The "unexhausted" can use their discretionary time to enhance their own lives and those of others, and combined activity with friends and family will diminish the isolation of modern life.

GET READY, GET SET, GO

The first ingredient in the constructive use of leisure leading to self-respect is *sufficient energy*. The next is being aware of the *need for self-motivation* and *direction*. We control our own activity and we must direct it, but we often shirk this task. Some men, exhausted, passive, or lazy after a week's (over)work want their spouses to lead them gently into leisure. Many Sunday athletes who don't want to be led or to think about alternatives simply grab their golf bags and head for the links or pick up their tennis rackets and go to the courts. Next to "resting," the major American leisure activity would seem to be chasing hard, soft, little, or big balls. Now, there's nothing wrong with this so long as it's balanced by other endeavors. The ancient Greeks knew plenty about leisure and they believed in a sound mind and a sound body. Far too many modern Americans put "body" first and foremost and consider sports the only possible leisure activity. They've lost the ancient "balance" of powers. It really doesn't matter how many push-ups Homer could do or how quickly Aristotle could skip rope—we assume their bodies were in good enough shape; we *know* them for their minds. When he wasn't jumping rope, Aristotle said that man's happiness lay in using his highest faculties well and in a manner of which he could be proud. All of which means enjoy your sports but use your mind too. Truly, more lasting values than volleying, tossing, kicking, or driving well must enter into how you spend the time you control.

LASTING VALUES:
PERSONAL AND SOCIAL

Personal value fulfillment means deriving knowledge, self-growth, and creative expression in your leisure time activities. You must decide what you want to do. Take an academic course, play a musical instrument, sing in the church choir, build furniture, read books...whatever; these are all personally fulfilling and lead you into the socially fulfilling stage. You can begin at home. Helping your own family is, like virtue, its own reward. From there you can move into community involvement. If you are politically minded, you can organize neighbors to clean up the environment or work for civic associations to clean up politics. Working against pollution and corruption could fill everyone's leisure time. If you're not an organizer, then use some other talent. Sportsmindedness per se is not a sin, particularly if you share your skill. Coach a Little League baseball team or play tennis with your kids. Those are only a couple of possibilities. The point is that any activity which gets you involved with others and is beneficial to them doesn't have to be all-consuming but will be rewarding. The rewards of a creative, intelligent use of leisure time really can compete with work rewards in every way except perhaps monetarily. In its own way, though, a well-spent leisure can be even *more* rewarding than work.

A neighbor of ours proved this point. He elected early retirement from an important Boston law firm for several reasons. He felt his company had grown too large and impersonal, he had been doing the same thing for thirty years, his pension would be adequate to his needs, and he wanted time to pursue his own interests. Having leisure time that he could control himself meant more to him than doing the bidding of and providing service to others. This is not to say he has become totally selfish. Far from it. Part of his full devotion to leisure includes working for several hospitals, sitting on various community boards and helping a number of charities. At the same time, he pursues his interest in nature, animals, birds, flowers, reading. He is free to develop new personal skills and to devote his time to family and friends. This man is no longer a washed-out, brief-cased basket case at the end of a work week, nor is he a retired "media-minded" zombie tied to the tube. He is, at last, self-motivated and enjoying every minute because his goals are now leisure-directed and attainable.

The good goals of leisure time should include personal growth, social service, religious and philosophical involvements, satisfying personal relations, ease and contentment, enjoyment and achievement. The more a person can achieve a proper fit between goals and behavior patterns, the better he will feel. "Taking it easy" is not really a prime leisure mode. Our neighbor is not taking it easy, he's simply doing it "his" way.

Leisure: Alone and Together

After you have made time for leisure and used it in a manner you can respect, the next problem is deciding how much leisure to spend with your spouse. Independence versus Togetherness is a predicament in all marriages. Men and women have social and solitary needs, and as they cater to one, the other grows. Every one of us desires to be both autonomous and gregarious. When we are alone for a while, we long to be with the rest of the family, when we are with the family, we soon yearn to be alone. It's quite natural. In dealing with the independence-togetherness question, "balance" is the key word.

There is a wonderful episode in Tchaikovsky's ballet *The Sleeping Beauty* called the "Rose Adagio." Princess

Aurora is introduced to a number of suitors, each of whom has brought her a rose. She is perched on her toes as one by one the young gallants step forward to make their presentations. They assist her in making a complete turn and then, always maintaining perfect balance, she lets go of the helping hand, raises her arms above her head, drops them gracefully and takes a rose from the suitor. When it's done well, it's a beautiful sight and a good lesson. The ballerina must know how and when to rely on the steady hand of her partners (togetherness) so that she can brace herself for her solo stance (independence). The one depends on the other. If you think it's easy, try it.

ALONE... WITH OTHERS

In addition to each person's need to be alone as opposed to with family, there is the question of leisure with friends and associates rather than with spouse and children. To spend discretionary time with others can be dangerous to a marriage because it implies rejection or inequality. We speak jokingly of golf, tennis, and sailing widows or widowers, but it's a heavy burden to be one of the great "abandoned" and it makes people angry. When one spouse is involved in an all-consuming activity, the problems of independent action versus togetherness can become extreme. Husbands and wives may become jealous of the other's activity or of each other's friends, the ones who "share" the time.

ALONE

Very often, productive and creative people of both sexes must isolate themselves from their families to accomplish what they have to do, but it is difficult for those who want to be alone to do so without making spouses feel unwanted. Too much autonomy ("I must be by myself") can become excessive and change a workable marriage into one in which the two partners live separately under one roof.

The best way to handle the apart-together question is to have respect for the other's leisure activity. Hurt feelings and misunderstandings can often be avoided by simple strategy. Those unwilling to give up any autonomy to the marriage are unlikely to have a satisfactory one, because commitment to marriage entails a willingness to modify self-interest and indulgence for the mutual benefit of the relationship. The alternative is to remain alone. Most people don't like being alone, so they are willing to make considerable compromise.

I DO, WE DO

Husbands and wives may feel guilty about leaving their partners alone and yet are miserable when they're together. They remain each other's leisure-time prisoners and can neither function happily apart nor harmoniously together. They need to confront the apart-together issue, establish priorities, and form agreements so they can use leisure in accordance with their principles. They must also realize that they cannot do everything together.

The good marriage is never a complete union in which the couple merge into one. Too much leisure-time sharing can result in lack of separate indentities. While it's important to share, it is equally important to have your own interests and friends apart from your spouse. If you are together all the time, there is nothing to tell each other. This can lead to boredom. Excessive dependence and inability to function alone don't help marriage. Couples incapable of independent action are, almost without exception, drags. Clinging vines went out with crinolines, so don't fall apart if your spouse takes off for a game of squash or a rubber of bridge—fill in the time with your own recreations but always be ready to come together. Be on tap.

After marriage, people remain individuals and husband and wife should face the fact they will struggle with "me" and "we" all their lives. That's why compromise is marriage's best friend. Couples can be totally incompatible in regard to leisure times, and in order to function as a team they have to make mutual concessions. For instance, one likes the beach, the other the mountains. One wants to travel, the other likes to unwind in one spot. When there are conflicts about where to go, what to do, and how to spend time, setting limits and living up to them helps immeasurably. "Okay, let's go to the seashore this summer and the mountains next," or "Come with me to the art museum for just an hour and I'll go to the movies with you." Once a "deal" is arranged, it should be respected. This summer's seashore *must* be next summer's mountains. It is far easier for the partner to "give" if he or she knows by experience that the other won't abuse the gift.

"LEISURING" TOGETHER

Those married in haste need not repent at leisure. Rather, couples can enjoy their leisure because the creative use of discretionary time enhances life together. Let yourself be introduced to your partner's favorite leisure-time activity. When an eminent stranger shows or tells you something, you look and listen in respectful silence; surely your husband or wife deserves the same chance—even more of one. You can expand your own knowledge and interests through your spouse's enthusiasm and instruction. Bear in mind that in a good marriage "leisuring" together is as essential as working together.

SEX

WE ARE BORN with our sexual organs wide awake. Controlled by the autonomic nervous system, they can operate without conscious direction. In fact, a male newborn produces spontaneous erections when *asleep!* But, spontaneity goes as the child grows. The sexual organs are taught to sleep, taught by parents, teachers, and society. The externally induced trance becomes an internal habit, especially in the mysterious female whose sexuality is largely invisible. (Her adult responses have now been viewed but her infant ones still cannot be seen.) Young men know pretty much what they've got and what to do with it, but young women can be ignorant of their own anatomy and 50 per cent never masturbate. A woman may not know how to give herself pleasure and cannot tell a man what she likes. If she is lucky, her partner will have learned elsewhere and will help in her self-awakening, but chance is not a reliable teacher and sensuality has slept through many marriages.

The situation has changed dramatically in the last thirty years. The researches of Alfred Kinsey, William Masters and Virginia Johnson, and others have awakened Americans to the facts of the facts of life. Although the researchers' names are household words, it is amazing how many people are still ignorant of their actual findings. In the laboratory Masters and Johnson showed that there is only one kind of female orgasm and it contains vaginal and clitoral aspects. During sexual relations, the clitoris can be stimulated directly by hand, mouth, or other means or indirectly during intercourse itself by pubic bone pressure or movement of the skin lying over it called the hood. The female climax is induced by stimulation of the clitoris and expressed by vaginal contractions. It is exactly analogous to the male response in which manipulation of the glans and shaft triggers reflex rhythmic contractions of the muscles at the base of the penis. It is now believed clitoral stimulation is necessary to arouse orgasm and this fact is supported by the observation that most self-manipulation by women is directed there.

The "clitoral revolution," part of the new knowledge of sex, has been accompanied by great attention and interest. Women want what they have been missing—a fair share of pleasure. They expect to be turned on and tuned in! As a result, dormant, sexless marriages are being shaken by the roots. Dutiful housewives, once willing to let their husbands satisfy themselves in "two minutes," now seek their rightful fulfillment, and established sexual styles in marriage are being uprooted.

Sexual Styles in Marriage

There are three types of sexual styles in marriage, the totally awake *passionate*, the completely asleep *sexless*, and the *mature/tender*.

THE PASSIONATE MARRIAGE

The passionate couple is the rarest of the three types and the partners most likely have been married recently. They've overcome the inhibitions set by parents, teachers, and society and their sensual alarm clock is constantly clanging. They vow never to slumber sexually again. They have reached the erotic "peak" and strain to remain in perpetual sexual motion. If their high is threatened, they become upset and may turn to artificial means to sustain it. Marijuana or cocaine is used in hopes of prolonging or heightening orgasm; numerous extra-marital partners may be sought to keep the thrill alive. But peaks are hard to maintain permanently—Romeo and Juliet cannot play the balcony scene forever. The desperate search for constant sexual excitement is bound to result in disappointment and resentment. Disappointment in oneself whenever the responsive fire fades and anger in the partner persistently called upon to fan the flame. The trouble with passionate marriages is that the I's must have it. Those whose spouses demand unending erotic excitement soon feel merely used because there is no tenderness, kindness, or thought of the partner—just an egocentric demand for the sensual sensational. Even if they both agree to try and sustain it, they'll begin to feel pressure. It is unnatural to live with such high performance expectation either in oneself or from another.

Passionate couples have an unrealistic, romantic notion about sex and marriage, but because of the great interest in the new sexual revolution, they are often envied by other couples who regard them as Sexual Joneses and want to keep up with them. While passionate couples seem to have achieved ideal, perfect sex every time and often, it is obviously not possible. These couples should not be envied. Far from it. Their lives are a strain as they try to live a myth, and if they aren't careful, they may revert to the next marital type, the sexless.

THE SEXLESS MARRIAGE:
THE GOOD, THE BAD, THE DISGUISED

The most unusual sexless union is one that is turned off from the start. For whatever reasons, it is literally never consummated. Celibate marriages exist, but most couples "have a go at it" and then, after a period of pre- and postmarital eroticism, lose lust. Usually ardor cools gradually, almost imperceptibly. The two may scarcely notice it's gone. They exhaust themselves with careers, the social whirl, children, household chores, maybe too much drinking, and don't realize what has happened. The "why" is never asked because the underlying sexual and marital difficulties are ignored. Sexual and marital disharmonies destroying desire include a list as long as the personal and interpersonal troubles between people. However, they are probably more genital than otherwise, because if *everything* between the couple were disastrous, the solution would be to terminate the marriage, not coitus. Since they chose to abstain from sexual intercourse and not from each other, it is likely that a major cause is carnal.

Once the romantic excitement that awakened their civilized sleeping sexual organs has passed, the years of repressive teaching may reassert influence. Sex is to be controlled. It is bad. The husband and wife begin to behave the way they were brought up. They've formed a new family but fall back into repressive sexual somnambulism and fall away from each other. There is, however, more to sex than intercourse.

The Good

Noncoupling couples can be warm, loving, affectionate, tender, and physically demonstrative. They may hold each other in bed and kiss. Indeed, they may be more sensual than those automatons who computer-coldly copulate for two minutes once or twice a week in accordance with the "national average." Ideally, it's best to have no hang-ups, but given the alternative between forgoing genital activity or loving tenderness, it is better to forgo the former. Genital inhibition is certainly not the worst marital problem, especially when the partners are in agreement. A sexless marriage of this type can be highly rewarding, extremely workable, satisfying, and stable.

Other nongenital unions may be even more sexless. Physical expression can be completely absent in marriage by mutual, perhaps unstated, agreement without either partner feeling deprived. Possibly they *ought* to feel cheated, but as long as they don't, the marriage can meet their other needs and be highly satisfying and satisfactory. No matter what their sexual style, most people rate nonerogenous wants above erogenous ones, so as long as both agree and feel no lack of lustful or tender expression, sexless unions present few problems. However, if the unbedded but happily wedded pair look around and see and hear how sexy our society is, they may become intimidated and want to keep up with the Erogenous Joneses. Pressure is felt by celibate couples when they hear everyone else is having multiple orgasms. They might begin to feel "odd" and perhaps attempt to discover if they *are* abnormal. They then test an outsider's reaction by consulting a doctor, counselor, or close friend, revealing they haven't slept together in a year and a half, and await the pronouncement. (We forget how strong the social attitude toward sexual behavior is in our post-Freudian world. In the old days, the family could have a "wonderful" bachelor uncle or a "helpful" spinster aunt. Now the family wonders, "Is he a homosexual? Is she frigid or lesbian?" The anthropologist Margaret Mead wisely noted that we tend to "sexualize everything" and this includes our relatives!)

If they are happy with their bedtime inactivity, sexless couples should not feel uncomfortable. Helping and loving each other are much more important than sex. It might also comfort them to know that celibate unions are more common than people realize or are willing to admit.

The Bad

Bad sexless marriages result when one or both partners are dissatisfied with the arrangement or enter into it for destructive reasons. If one or both crave genital contact that is denied because of fear, anger, or the wish to avoid disappointment, strong stress on the union ensues. Lack of intercourse is, then, not a mutual understanding—it's a symptom of a "cold war" and the marriage is in trouble. As sexual frustration grows, irritability increases; the couple becomes even more upset and the situation worsens. Sexless marriages of this type are unstable. Partners must resolve differences in *and* out of bed or they are in danger of splitting.

The Disguised

The most common variety of nonerotic wedlock is the disguised sexless marriage. Couples attempt to (and often succeed in) fooling themselves and each other into believing they are being sexual when they really are not. Relations are performed in hasty, superficial, and routine manner with little love, tenderness, joy, or pleasure. The primary aim is to "do it." The dosage is steady, but the satisfaction is meager and the couple is left unfulfilled.

Periods of disguised sexlessness do not always represent serious marital difficulty but can result from external stress and strain. A man or woman worried about his or her career may feel decidedly *un*sexy and yet, recognizing the needs of the partner and not wanting to deny him or her, goes through perfunctory relations. The one on the receiving end of this "relative" indifference is supposed to understand, but it can be a source of eventual strife. One doesn't want excuses. One wants love and good sex.

Sexlessness also can be a phase in marriage—a reversion to puritan type following initial passion, a period when little babies or career worries distract—or it can be an angry withdrawal.

Sex: Do You Need It?

Partners who are upset by sexless marriages should stop and think why they are in one. Do they have personal sexual problems or marital difficulties or are pressures from the outside world to blame? At what point did the union become sexless, what caused the change, and how long has it been going on? If for years, why has each partner allowed it to continue? Have they both become used to and comfortable with a bad sexless marriage? Perhaps they feel it gives them *cartes blanches* to seek other bed partners or to stay out until all hours at the office. Does it provide one partner with a reason for righteous indignation toward the other? Those too dependent on their mates can use sexlessness to make them feel independent and "grown up." Some partners can only cease clinging to each other by getting angry, stopping sex, and withdrawing.

Sometimes the physical drive is not strong and a person is happier without intercourse, but even if the drive is there, sexual inhibition and ignorance can make coitus a calamity. Partners worried because they're not "making it" physically every night have to adjust their sights. They must exercise patience and understanding and communicate with each other so they can achieve and participate in a mature/tender marriage.

THE MATURE/TENDER MARRIAGE

The mature/tender sexual marriage neither "strains" for the thrill of first love nor indulges in too many periods of sexlessness. This union seeks to meet the emotional and genital needs of each partner. Based on sensitive knowledge of the likes and dislikes of husband and wife, it strives for kindness, warmth, and excitement.

Men and women, aware of their own anatomy and that of their lovers, have no problem giving and receiving pleasure. They delight in it. They aim for great sexual peaks and reach them because of how well they know each other and how deeply they care, yet they wisely accept lesser pleasures especially when life impinges. They know they cannot achieve romantic, passionate, adolescent wonder woman-superman levels when overtired, worried about finances, or disturbed by the children. A tender marital lover considers the other's full life, not some separate, detached sexual performance or standard. The difference between one partner's own likes and those of the other causes no impatience. When necessary, allowances are made in the full knowledge that the next time or next month it will be better—maybe the best!

THE TRI-CYCLE BUILT FOR TWO

The three sexual styles of marriage—passionate, sexless, and mature/tender—can all occur in the same marriage . . . and usually do. A marriage starts out passionate and then becomes sexless, or relatively so, when partners are faced with marital changes and outside worries. Later, sexlessness should give way to a mature/tender relationship that includes exciting and emotionally fulfilling love-making. But sexless periods may recur—in fact, married people could save themselves a lot of misery if they realized cycles are inevitable. Passion cannot last forever and sexlessness probably won't. At those times when a deprived spouse gets upset and angry, expressions of hostility should be tolerated and the partner should try to respond by givng what their lover has a right to expect.

The Ways to Mature/Tender Matrimony

At certain moments *all* married partners do bad things to each other in bed. Stop and think of what it takes to achieve tender yet exciting conjugal sex, and you'll realize there are no exceptions. Assuming the pair has mastered inventive, personally pleasing techniques, time and energy still must be taken to practice them. Good erotic functioning can be sabotaged by the erosions of daily life: the angry boss, the sick child, money worries, ill health. In addition, there is the inevitability of marital strife. One of Freud's greatest formulations is his concept of ambivalence, a combination of love and hate existing in all long-term relationships, including marriage. Anger at your spouse occurs over annoying habits, insensitivities, frustrations, competition... causes as endless as their effects. These inevitable negative emotions have to affect the physical relationship. Sexual problems are usually due to marital strife rather than to poor love-making techniques. In fact, sex therapists who instruct in "mechanics only" are finding suitable cases rarer and rarer. Though most people now know what to do, they are often too angry to get on with it. One thirtyish housewife in therapy attended a sex therapy clinic and was thoroughly instructed in how to pleasure her husband. By the time she finished, she was a walking *Kamasutra*. However, she stopped using all her techniques almost immediately because, as she told her analyst, "I can't stand to see him so excited after the way he treats me!" All the technique in the world wouldn't sweeten that relationship. Solving the underlying animosity is what really was required.

DON'T BE SUPERSENSITIVE

Worldly worries and marital strife persistently "crawl" beneath the covers on the marriage bed, but don't let your partner's occasional boudoir nastiness get you down. Favorite ways for married partners to snipe at each other include the husband's implying the wife is frigid, too inhibited, and not really interested in sex, while she calls him an insensitive animal who uses her body to masturbate. Pretty harsh stuff? These are just a few of the comments some couples shout at each other or think while pretending to be pleasant. If you're on the receiving end of the barbs, don't discount all the kind words previously uttered and don't jump to the conclusion that your husband or wife *really* believes what he or she says. Your partner is only human, loves you some times, hates you others, or perhaps is just plain tired and grouchy. The fact is that wedded lovers can't afford to be too sexually sensitive. Everyone's genital organs are affected by daily stresses, but some people's are too delicately responsive. If you're one of those people, you're losing the opportunity to use them to escape from life's miseries, to come out of yourself, and to float away with your partner in pleasure. Don't make the mistake of waiting for the *perfect* moment for sex. Everything between you and your partner or you and the outside world doesn't have to be A-okay in order for the two of you to copulate. On the contrary, sex can be used to help you forget squabbles and troubles as you please your partner and yourself.

DON'T WORRY ABOUT POTENCY OR ORGASM

Every man worries about his potency on occasion; some worry all the time. Is his erection hard enough? Will it go away? Does he ejaculate on time? Is he fast or slow? Does he please his wife?

The reaction to sexual mishaps can be much more a problem than the occurrence itself. The man who failed to get an erection last time frets about *this* time. It makes him far less likely to become hard than if he focused on receiving and giving erotic pleasure. In fact, the cornerstone for the treatment of erectile difficulties is to help the man concentrate on the pleasing sensations in his penis rather than worry about whether it will be able to perform.

Every woman is concerned on occasion about having an orgasm and many women worry all the time. Will it be clitoral or vaginal? Will it be strong enough? Will her vagina be moist and responsive? Will she please her husband?

Except when a woman's organs do not lubricate and dilate, her sexual functioning is a lot less obvious than a man's. A woman achieves orgasm through knowledge of her anatomy and the co-operation of her partner in stimulating and satisfying her. For her problems, concentration on receiving pleasure plus recognition of any angry wishes to exclude her husband are major steps in overcoming sexual difficulties.

Married couples do well to recognize good and bad sexual encounters and take them in stride. One advantage is knowing each other well and being aware of previous ups and downs. New, unmarried lovers feel much more pressure to prove themselves and often flounder. Sometimes they seek advice between the covers of a book for problems that occur between the sheets. However, the best way to achieve good mature/tender marital sex is not to buy a book on where and how to stroke each other but to realize you are not mechanical dolls in a text. You are two human beings who probably already know how to thrill one another and still run into occasional snags or destructive interactions.

Defending Against
Destructive Interaction:
Sexual and Nonsexual

Marital sex life can be ruined by sexual ignorance and shyness, by underlying guilt and antisexual feelings, and by angry carry-overs outside the bedroom. The best way to improve is to identify the source of your trouble accurately.

THE SEXUAL

Most families have stronger feelings about loss of virginity in females than in males. It's the farmer's daughter we worry about, not his son. Because most women can now control pregnancy, this attitude may change in time, but up until now girls have grown up more repressed and ignorant of how to attain sexual pleasure than boys. In addition, those who learn later in life are sometimes too embarrassed to ask their husbands for what would please them. Shyness and ignorance conspire to ruin the married woman's sex life. It is here a husband can help. If a wife is unable to speak out, the husband should "explore" her, keeping his eyes and ears open for signs of response. When he gets them, the actions that elicited the response should be repeated in the future. It's very important for a man not to be angry at his spouse for being repressed and shy. Women too should remember that men can also be "innocent," in which case, she should take the initiative and go on an erotic exploration of her husband.

THE UNCONSCIOUS

Sexual revolutions don't happen overnight. For five
thousand years, the Judeo-Christian tradition has
preached that sex is only acceptable for procreation. The
world's longest, steadiest sermon cannot be erased in one
generation. Guilt and the feeling that sex for pleasure is
wrong still exist even in the most enlightened. These
deep-seeded attitudes still flower and prevent thousands
of couples from enjoying full erotic pleasure. Rather than
look for a magic charm or clinic to rub out all
unconscious religious and historic influences, it makes
more sense for us to tolerate the quaint remnants of
inhibition in ourselves and our partners. It's only human
to denounce our spouses angrily for their lack of sexual
freedom, but it's smarter to lead them gently away from
those old ideas. Understanding and co-operation will go a
long way in overcoming them.

THE NONSEXUAL
DESTRUCTIVE INFLUENCES ON SEX

Using the bed as a battlefield in an attempt to prove one's
partner frigid, impotent, insensitive, boorish, or unattractive is bad. It's absolutely the wrong place to tear each
other down or continue on-going power struggles. *Don't
express anger in bed.* Alas, for all of us, it's easier said
than done. When it happens, as it inevitably will, forgive
and forget. Don't carry a grudge. If you become so furious
you have to refuse sex, be honest and say so. Chances are
your spouse is angry too and is perhaps offering sex as a
conciliatory gesture. By the way, it might not be a bad
idea to go along with your spouse once in a while and
enjoy a falling in instead of a falling out.

Who's Afraid of the Big Bad Affair?

"Thou shalt not commit adultery."

"Thou shalt not covet thy neighbor's wife."

Those are two of the Ten Commandments and *both* are on the same subject, so we may safely assume it's always been a big temptation. Moses did carry down from Mount Sinai wise stone directives. It's best not to have affairs. Today we're afraid of them because they hurt our partner's feelings, threaten trust, cause jealousy, and can seriously harm our marriages.

Affairs seem to provide what marriages may lack—romantic love apart from reality and strife, a holiday from responsibility, and even a kind of immortality. In his poem *Adultery* James Dickey writes of "rooms we cannot die in" where "gigantic forepleasure lives..." But the poet later acknowledges, "Nothing can come of this, nothing can come of us..." Illicit relationships may provide delightful escapes, but they also exact harsh reckonings. They happen because we're, again, only human. We err because we want to escape reality, and we thoughtlessly, selfishly enjoy the moment without considering the morrow.

HOW DID IT HAPPEN?

Most married people don't intend to have affairs; in fact, they try to avoid them. When they happen, they are, they're convinced, "accidents." But, the final decision to have sexual intercourse with someone is always deliberate and not to be blamed on alcohol or a moment's madness. It is an accident only in the sense that a person may have grown close to someone gradually and unintentionally developed increasingly strong erotic feelings. This is usually a result of propinquity to close friends, neighbors, or fellow workers. Most affairs occur on the job, with a wife's or husband's best friend, or with a couple with whom husband and wife socialize. To avoid such "accidents," you have to be aware of what's going on. Don't see too much of that attractive couple or work too closely late and alone with that sensitive, bright, good-looking someone on the job.

Desire for an attractive new man or woman is a perfectly normal thing. There is a promise of adventure, fun, and excitement and the daily realities are forgotten. Sex organs deadened by strife and the inevitable marital ambivalences may function proud and moist with someone new for whom there is only positive feeling. If you've had an affair under such circumstances in the past, watch out for repeated "accidents." They may just be a way for you to avoid facing the fact that you like affairs and are on the prowl for one.

Also, affairs are more of a temptation at some points in life than others. Know this and you'll be on guard at critical times: when your husband becomes busier after a promotion or when your wife is preoccupied with a new baby or job. In all these instances, a gram of prevention is worth a kilo of cure.

HOW MUCH DOES
THE AFFAIR THREATEN MARRIAGE?

Affairs can be anything from casual dalliances after the office Christmas party to deep loves breaking up marriages. How intense or how threatening they are is somewhat but not entirely under the participant's control—hence the danger. Unless both partners are extramaritally occupied, a married couple in the "throes of an affair" can be divided into two camps, active and passive. The active person is having the affair while the passive one is not and may or may not know what's going on. While we have no intention of writing a handbook for affairs, if one is going on, there are certain things which can be done to limit the threat to marriage, and that *is* our concern.

The Active Partner

Obviously, the active partner has trouble with rules and has already ignored one fifth of the Ten Commandments. Still, if one partner is involved in an affair, we propose another list—this time five don'ts.

1. *Don't Fall in Love*. Married people are used to caring, tender sex and often can't help but bring the same intensity to extramarital relationships. It's very tempting to fall in love—for some, it makes the sensual that much more exciting and meaningful; for others it makes the affair seem less immoral. But don't confuse momentary passion for love and don't allow love to unseat temporary lust.

2. *Don't Confess*. If you have an urge to come clean by word or deed because you feel guilty, let those scruples help you *stop* the illicit alliance rather than make a confession. Telling may clear your conscience, but it may also hurt your spouse unnecessarily.

3. *Don't Pick Anyone Too Needy or Crazy*. A lonely, sad single who wants you all the time (including major holidays) will exert severe pressure on your marriage. If you have found an emotionally disturbed person who looks to you to make things all better, you have an explosive situation on your hands and a serious threat to your marriage. In both cases, choosing such lovers in an attempt to have a little adventure or fun is an act of cruelty, not love.

4. *Don't Lose Perspective*. An affair won't save your

life or make you happy. It might provide a little excitement or diversion, but it can't be your renaissance. It can't even make you a new, sensitive person if you aren't one anyway.

5. *Don't Overlook the Effect on Your Spouse.* Will your affair make him or her desperately unhappy or will it be taken in stride? No affair is worth sending your partner into a profound, long-lasting depression, hurting someone you love, and filling your marriage with endless mistrust and recrimination.

The Passive Spouse

The partner who is cheated on is likely to feel hurt and unhappy, and the question of vigilance can't help but arise. Some married people, overly conscious of the threat of infidelity, are constantly on their guard, suspiciously searching, snooping, and querying. Such behavior creates an unpleasant atmosphere in the home and does little good either in arresting ongoing infidelity or in preventing its onset. Therefore we advise against excessive detective work. On the other hand, one can be too naïve. It's not necessary to be Sherlock Holmes, but you don't have to be an eternal victim either. If your partner stops showing any interest in you sexually or keeps "odd" hours, the chances are an affair might be the cause. What you don't know may not hurt you, but such behavior is an obvious (though sometimes unconscious) invitation for you to ask some tough questions.

If you discover your partner's infidelity, don't take it too personally. Of course, you can't help having certain reactions, but what we mean is, don't think it really reflects on your physical attractiveness, how good you are in bed, or how loved and valued you are. Too many men and women subscribe to the myth that if they were okay, their partners wouldn't stray. It's just not true. Many beautiful, perfect wives have unfaithful husbands, and doting, caring, perfect husbands can be casually cuckolded.

In most cases, just as they marry such individuals, people are likely to have affairs with those to whom they are geographically and emotionally close. That's why you should never get "hung up" on *who* the person is. Since propinquity plays an important role, it probably will be a neighbor, friend, or co-worker of your husband or wife.

Realizing your problem can make it somewhat easier to bear; then you can work on it. Think about your own marriage before this happened, and if you feel it is worth saving, then be patient. If your partner has "broken the rules" and fallen in love, give him or her time to get over it and be prepared for difficulties. It is very hard to live with someone passionately involved with another, but passion fades and time is on your side. Chances are that what you and your spouse had together is more valuable and long-lasting and will survive what for the moment seems like an irresistible threat.

Active and Passive Resistance

People should split because of bad, irreparable marriages, not because of affairs. With our increasing life spans, marriages can last many years. During this extended period, there's a fifty-fifty chance one or both partners will have an affair or two. This means both partners must try to be cool and levelheaded during those ordeals. The active spouse shouldn't blindly assume the new lover is superior, and the passive one shouldn't take it as a statement of lack of personal worth. Both should work to save the marriage, the active by making proper and believable amends, the passive by accepting and forgiving.

Sex and Marriage

The marriage contract implies expectation of sexual gratification. When this is not fulfilled anger and frustration may result. The trouble with expectation is that spontaneous pleasure and joy can be replaced by grim duty. People rebel. Good sex is not a marital right; it is a delicate skill. It cannot be taken for granted but requires reasonable attention.

ATTENTION MUST BE PAID

This means you ought to think about how your sex life is going—not all the time, but sometimes. There are, after all, other things in your marriage perhaps even more important and you cannot think of everything all the time. But, it's as dangerous to ignore sex as to be preoccupied by it.

Some couples focus too much on sex. One reason is the mistaken notion that if the bed is perfect, everything else in their lives will be. Sex is often falsely blamed for any marital discord, but even when the physical aspects seem settled, unrelated problems won't go away, and couples soon learn that marriage is bigger than the bed.

It is, however, more common to pay too little attention to sex, especially after the marriage has gone on for a while. Normally, sexless periods occur when one or both partners are too busy, tired, or worried to think of anything but job, money, or kids. Marital sex, eroded by boredom, bad feelings, worries of all kinds, requires periodic refreshing—cool bursts of attention.

What is the right amount of attention to pay to your marital sex life? Actually, it is the appropriate measure for your particular marriage, the quality and quantity that makes you feel comfortable and that continues tender close communication with your partner. How much is that? Everyone is different, but each marriage has its own rhythm and partners sense when it is off. When you feel too detached from your partner, tell him or her. If your partner doesn't hear, you may have to shout. If he or she still doesn't or can't respond, you may have to be patient... but not for too long. Don't try to be a saint. Shout again.

HOME IMPROVEMENTS ARE POSSIBLE

We have been impressed by how many married people suffer sexually and have no hope for improvement. Perhaps some of them "hide" behind a wall of hopelessness in order to avoid their partner, but some genuinely believe sexual behaviors cannot change. There is absolutely no need to feel hopeless about marital sex life. Want proof? Below is a list of Masters and Johnson's cure rates for sexual problems:

Impotence	74%
Premature ejaculation	98%
Retarded ejaculation	60%
Inorgastic women	83% (improved or cured)
Vaginismus (spastic vagina)	100%

We will not enter into a precise technical discussion of the methods used or the exact significance of these figures. The point here is that the numbers show hope! You don't *have* to suffer through a sexually troubled marriage. The two of you can *do* something to improve it.

Pay attention to what you and your partner like and do so in correct balance. Avoid self-observation, judgment, worry over failure, humiliation, and performance anxiety. Those who concentrate on their own pleasure have spouses who feel used and frustrated, while those who concentrate on pleasing miss their own erotic self-joy. Relax, involve yourself, and pleasure will substitute for fear.

TAKE TIME AND ENERGY FOR SEX

Tender physical intimacy cannot be achieved in the last drunken gasp on a Saturday night or as a worn-out automatic move after a long work day. Once in a while, make time for your love life—put sex first instead of last. This is exactly what sex therapies advocate and they suggest all sorts of techniques. One of the most successful is "sensate focusing." One partner lies down while the other languidly and delicately touches the partner from head to toe, from front to back and then they switch. Each is instructed to concentrate on the pleasure experienced. The result is an erect penis and a dilated vagina simply because sex has been put first.

Declare an evening for sex just as you would for the movies or doing income taxes. Use sensate focusing, change the location or lighting, go away, do anything you want. We don't have a lot of faith in external stimulation, but it does help many people. Sometimes when the delicate balance between taking and giving sexual pleasure has been upset in the direction of giving or receiving too much, different "exercises" like those mentioned can restore it. Sensitivity to your partner, variety, a willingness to listen, asking for what you like, all these will help keep your marital sexuality alive.

EXPERIMENT

Being experimental is not only a great cure for bedroom boredom; it also shows your partner you care. It's an expression of love and willingness to be close and intimate.

People are often afraid to try something "new." They kid themselves into thinking they are sexually free but avoid the different. Dull repetition makes them secure. They fear the "new" may be perverted or dirty, and vestiges of old-fashioned inhibitions surface. We don't want anyone to do anything that will cause them pain or disgust, but remember, sometimes such anticipation is really anxiety and sexual guilt in disguise. Accommodating your partner doesn't mean going through the same old routine; it means helping him or her to be comfortable enough to ask you to do the "thrilling" thing they want without fear of ridicule or chastisement. Lovers shouldn't be dead set on scoring a bull's-eye on the genital target; they should try to achieve physical intimacy without worry and one way is by being open to experiment. For example, the mature couple knows that the largest sexual organ of the body is . . . the skin. Harald Schultz-Hencke, an early psychoanalyst, considered sexuality to be rooted in the genitals and tenderness in the skin. We now know genital tenderness and cutaneous sensuality also exist, and couples can use this knowledge to great advantage as they work to pleasure one another.

COMMUNICATE

Verbalizing intimate feelings and desires promotes closeness and trust in *all* ways. If you stop power struggles, childishness, and frustration in bed, you'll co-operate better nonsexually. While bad sex leads to bad intimacy, it does not follow that good sex leads to good intimacy, but sensual fufillment sure helps.

To communicate effectively you must pay attention to what you like and learn what your partner likes. Your saying "You haven't touched me there in ten years" makes your partner defensive rather than desire to please you. It would be better to say "Please touch me like this" without the accusation about previous failure. It would be nice if your spouse were willing to tell you the same in a direct manner, but some people find it very difficult to do so. While you can never read the other's mind or do as well as you would if he or she said what was wanted, you may be able to do a little better if you try and become a "keen observer."

Those who try to overcome shyness may seem awkward and even aggressive in their request for pleasure. In general, demands and commands make the recipient want to rebel and say no. It is better to say, "I love it when you do this with your tongue," than to roughly push the partner's head and say, "Do this!" Therefore, concentrate on how you ask for what you want. If you feel angry that your partner has been so insensitive all these years as to have forgotten or not learned what you like, chances are you'll make your request in an aggressive manner. Try to calm yourself down and then ask for what you want, without recrimination for what hasn't been done.

Finally, pay attention to what turns you off, makes you tense, and causes your mind to wander. Tell your partner. Airing your complaints and concerns will improve your erotic life immeasurably.

THE GLORIES OF MARITAL SEX

Marital sex is the best sex and includes delicate communication between a husband and wife wishing to give and receive pleasure.

In humans, sex is largely governed by the brain. It is not just "wham-bam" time but time for talk and communication. The proof is that the same sexual activity can be extremely satisfying with one for whom you care and desire and unsatisfying with someone you fear or dislike. Physiological orgasm may be achieved in each instance, but in the first instance it will produce pleasure and aid intimacy while in the latter it brings lingering guilt and shame. The "connection" between married lovers is not just a physical one.

On the average, married couples have more sex than singles—almost any time they want it. If you find yourself envious of the rough-and-ready sex of the "unattached," stop and consider the alienation and emptiness of promiscuity. Sex without caring, intimacy, and friendship is depressing, shallow, and fleeting. The cold flame of momentary passion loses intensity, and the ability to distinguish one emotional situation from another is also lost. Married people know each other so well that they can give and receive more sexual pleasure than strangers offer. A whore "turns a trick"—a loving partner stirs deep emotions bringing in concepts of personal relationship, responsibility, sharing, and loving. Sex serves to attach a couple further to each other.

Smart couples value the stability and companionship of home. When tempted to stray, they understand that people tend to take what they have for granted, including sex with a spouse. They understand, too, that people crave what they don't have and they know about the lure of the unknown and the compelling tug of "curiosity." But, mature married couples also realize that outside sex intensifies feelings of jealousy and possessiveness. They know "open marriages" don't work. (The authors of the original book on that subject have admitted it themselves, and even radical Swedish communes have had to impose anti-promiscuity rules!) Though couples may occasionally be touched by the lingering longing for the romantic forbidden, smart ones fight it off. Yes, it is difficult at times to stay home and be satisfied, but it is a great comfort to have a home.

Finally, marital sex is less pressured than single or adolescent sex and is more likely to be free of silly performance anxiety. Although the wise partners know enough not to be lazy, they don't have to conduct a frantic sideshow at every coupling. It is a loving act with a margin for error and room for compassion. They are less embarrassed with each other and can request what they like in bed even if it seems strange.

Successfully married people enjoy sex together as intimacy more than as intercourse. Comfort and acceptance are as appreciated as "thrills." They touch and hold each other. They know family life is the strongest bulwark against the isolation and anonymity of modern urban life and they cling to one another. The marital sexual balance is a delicate one to maintain, but it is a strong and beautiful bond between two people.

FIGHTS

The sleepless nights, the endless fights
    The quick toboggan when you reach the heights
I miss the kisses and I miss the bites
    I wish I were in love again...

IN THIS Rodgers and Hart ballad, lyricist Lorenz Hart accurately put his finger on the rapidly beating pulse of a love affair. The lyric, however, describes a courtship, not a long-term relationship, a preliminary rather than a main event. Lovers' quarrels with themselves and the world are ever the same, and a brand new relationship, like virgin territory, must be explored. Tossing in bed at night, fighting over "nothing," passion, pain, highs, lows, ups, downs—all are telescoped into vivid, ever-exciting encounters of lovers in order to feel each other out. Fighting is a means of testing to see if a commitment can endure. But once the affair culminates in marriage, different regulations are imposed.

Control Your Emotions

When it comes to marital disagreements, some individuals continue to regard emotion and action as inseparable. It's not so! Except for the excessively impulsive, actions do not automatically result from feelings. Even hostile passions can be tempered by understanding the reasons why you are upset, by distracting your mind from them, or busying yourself with other matters until you calm down. If you are angry, you don't have to express it. For instance, when an aggressive juvenile delinquent is insulted, he's liable to leap from the depths of the blackboard jungle and attack like a wild animal. If, on the other hand, a senior partner humiliates a young associate, the beginner is likely to retreat into the executive suite maze saying and doing nothing against his superior. He may experience the same intense anger as the adolescent but he chooses to keep it inside and not act. It's usually a wise move; yet even as he acts demurely the poor fellow is probably convinced he'll get an ulcer from bottling up his emotions—he won't, and, what's more, he'll keep his job.

IGNORE THE MODERN MESSAGE

The peculiar notion that keeping quiet is bad for your health, especially if you are angry, is the modern rallying cry. Suppressing or disguising negative emotions such as fear, anger, and jealousy is supposed to strongly increase your chances for physical or psychological illness. Squashing aggressive urges has been implicated as the cause of a miasma of troubles including anxiety, ulcers, depression, and heart attacks. It takes the blame for everything—quite possibly the reason why the Mets don't win the pennant.

So much of the literature supports this "let-it-all-hang-out-or-it-will-eat-you-up" view, it's hard not to heed the message. One pair of authors actually suggested couples have a *Who's Afraid of Virginia Woolf* "free-for-all, no verbal-holds barred, below the beltline insult exchange" to clear the air and help the relationship. This theory was very highly touted, but why wasn't it noted that the endless fight between George and Martha in the Edward Albee play was a destructive catharsis leaving the characters and the audience drained and stunned. What kind of model is this for behavior when the results are so disastrous? Despite the dangerous consequences, those authors, like so many others, willy-nilly recommend "expressing yourself fully." And to whom do they assign this theory?... Sigmund Freud!

EXPRESS THYSELF—BUT THINK FIRST

Freud said psychological symptoms are caused by the repression of unacceptable impulses. He gave, as one example, an adult woman taking exclusive care of an aged parent at the expense of her own freedom and unable to express or acknowledge resentment. When the parent died, the daughter became melancholic for an extended period of time. Using this story and similar examples as texts, some have carried Freud's idea to extremes of absurdity, implying that every little squelched feeling leads to mental or physical illness. Like the Freudian example of the "dutiful daughter," they claim we'll wind up all wound up if we don't let go immediately. This is a ridiculous assumption. The originator of psychoanalysis himself was quite aware of the necessity to *delay*, even *repress*, expression of a strong feeling and to put it in acceptable form before releasing it. Instant discharge of angry feelings can make you as sick or sicker than excessively inhibiting them, but popular psychologists have latched onto a distorted view and refuse to let go of their misinterpretation: "Pop off," say the "popsychos."

POPSYCHOS VERSUS VICTORIANISM:
BEWARE FALSE NOTIONS

In a frantic attempt to be anti-Victorian, popular psychologists recommend a welter of active remedies including fights. Their reasoning is simple...too simple. Victorians repressed sex and emotion: *bad!* Expressing sex and emotion, part of the new freedom, is healthy and will make you grow: *good!* Greatgrandma said, "Masturbation causes madness!" Her enlightened descendant counters, "Lack of masturbation causes madness!" In their efforts to ice the treacle of past beliefs, the Popsychos go from one absurdity to another.

In marriage as well, many "experts" have renounced reserved behavior in favor of letting it all hang out. If you're angry, say so! Particularly if you're angry at your spouse. No more delicate interference from society, which once clearly defined male and female role behavior and decreed that sex be performed for procreation not pleasure. Today couples are supposedly "free" to choose their own way, but in fact, thanks to the Popsychos, society is even pushier. Couples who want to consider themselves "normal" had better have a wild time in bed, alternate who does the cooking, and fight with one another.

While Popsychos advocate fighting to prevent mental and physical illness, no one has ever shown that shouting or fighting clears the marital air. Furthermore, though it's not known how much squabbling is "normal," some authors blithely suggest that every couple should have two to three fights per week, as though they were prescribing medication or suggesting the correct number of sexual encounters. People then feel compelled to keep up with a nonexistent norm. Yes, there is fighting in marriage, but there is no "proper" frequency for it, and should a national statistical average ever be published...ignore it!

STALE MATES

Though fighting between intimates is normal, there are certain couples who don't fight—just about all their problems have been ironed out because they've been married so long and function so well as a team. It's rare ... slightly suspect ... but possible. In general, however, no tiffs is a good tip-off something is wrong. Partners tiptoeing around each other out of indifference or fear have soft-shoed themselves into a corner of married splitdom. After all, strangers don't feel enough strong emotions to cause them to wrangle, and if you and your mate are distant enough, there may be little or no friction. It's hardly anything to brag about. There is no joy for anyone watching partners at each other's throats all the time, but pleasure is similarly stillborn when one listens to the self-satisfied smugly declare, "Oh we *never* fight!"

It is natural to experience anger and it cannot be wholly suppressed, but anger in marriage must be *managed*—neither allowed to become too great nor so guarded against as to disappear. In order to reach intimacy, you have to be able, as Erik Erikson wrote, "to engage in controversy and useful combat."

How Not to Fight: Shut Up

Empty marital battles don't necessarily clear the air; they may just as easily foul it. In the majority of cases, fights shatter the emotional tranquillity of the home, interfere with sleep, digestion, productivity, and leave permanent scars. Quarrels are inevitable, but when they occur they should be channeled into "useful combat." To do this, you must actually pick the time as carefully as you pick the fight and it must be when you are *not* out of control.

Though we champion marital disarmament and unilateral peace on the home front, we are aware that the inevitable flash of anger arises. When it does, we advise you to *shut up*—but don't keep quiet forever. While your temper is on "hold," you can time and soften your response, making it an effective tool in eliminating the problem that aroused your ire. It is possible that results can only be attained through a battle and therefore we are not suggesting you never fight—merely that you avoid the automatic, reflexive, unproductive *constant* varieties: those causing your spouse to become defensive and unyielding and those preventing you from getting your partner to alter the behavior that annoyed you in the first place. And don't worry about your health. Being quiet will *not* give you high blood pressure, depression, or ulcers. On the contrary, it can preserve your domestic tranquillity and improve your health. Shutting up is literally a pause that refreshes.

LEARNING NOT TO FIGHT

The "expressive scream" school of psychology may believe that consistently repressed anger leads to empty marriages, but it doesn't have to. You don't go through life screaming at strangers, superiors, friends, and colleagues, so why store it up for your spouse? (To be truthful, most of us don't. In a psychiatric office the few cases of marital screamers are small-minded men and women who want to yell at work but content themselves by shrieking at their families at home because they can get away with it there without being fired or arrested.) Reflex fighting is the *modus operandi* of the *bellum conjugale*. Avoid it by controlling yourself and remembering three quick ways to stay out of senseless marital fights:

1. When you are in a bad mood or temper, tell your partner and give fair warning of your stormy state.

2. Even better, try to repair yourself rather than rely entirely on your spouse to cheer you up. Relieve anger through activities other than fighting. Work in the yard, clean the house, go out and jog, meditate, play a musical instrument; let aggression diffuse into leisure and soothe your own bad feelings. Your partner isn't running an emotional McDonald's and cannot do it all for you.

3. Don't blame your spouse for your bad mood. Catch yourself when you too readily and wrongly attribute your distress to the person closest at hand.

Develop the Delayed Shut-Up

Sometimes people genuinely do not realize they're in a bad mood until after they've made a nasty crack. This is a good time for the delayed shut-up. Once the first salvo has been fired, stop and think. There is still time to halt the impending war by offering a simple "Sorry, I've had a hard day and I'm tired," or "That was uncalled for—forgive me." Chances are the other person will be satisfied and not fight back. Then, if you continue in mild-to-mean doldrums, go into another room and either reason it out or distract yourself with mindless or pleasant activity.

LEARN TO LIVE WITH TENSION

Like stinging BB shots, angry remarks and curt rejoinders ricochet through matrimony. Television, the mini-mirror of our lives, makes the most of the potentially comic dialogue in marital "rat-tat-tats." "All in the Family," "Maude," "The Jeffersons"—most situation comedies are based on conjugal pugnaciousness and snappy retorts—a source radio plumbed for years. One radio series was actually called "The Bickersons." Argumentative to a fault, Mr. and Mrs. Bickerson held the mirror up to the audience, which responded, as it does today, with the laughter of recognition. Onlookers can afford to giggle, but participants in real home battles don't find it funny. It's hard to live under a barrage of sarcastic one-liners, and it's equally difficult to keep from firing them off yourself. The way to do it is to make allowances. Hold *yourself* back a little and either learn to overlook thoughtless, meaningless jabs from your partner or answer back without getting too upset and escalating the verbal skirmish into full-fledged combat. In other words, *learn to live with a little tension*. Laboring under the misapprehension that your work day is unbearably stressful, that you're fed up and can't "take anymore," sets you up to expect the impossible from marriage: perfect harmony.

Having been a responsible, hard-working, charming adult all day, you may be tempted to come home and release the stored up aggression of the day plus more on your spouse. If a man expects summa-cum-laude service and attention at home because his job is so high-pressure, he really is asking too much. It makes more sense under such circumstances to change to a lower-pressure job than to change spouses in an effort to find the paragon who doesn't exist. Wives, too, can react in infantile fashion. Babyish fighters of both sexes let all aggressions and hurt feelings pour forth over the smallest matter. Is the toothpaste cap on or off? Who left the dirty socks on the floor? Why is the garbage piled up? Why wasn't this put away . . . that thrown out? Why isn't dinner ready? From morning to night nothing is overlooked, everything is grist for the mill, and the couple responds to every stimulus as marriage becomes a show-and-tell of trivia. Ultimately, it is less painful to put the cap on the tube or pick up dirty socks and dump them in the hamper than to have long senseless squabbles about neatness. No one wins in these petty fights, and if you learn to *shut up*, you won't be troubled by small matters. Save yourself for the important issues so you can be heard. Truly, shutting up helps one maintain perspective.

The point, already made but no less sharp, is that partners have to conserve some charm and patience for each other. Yet even if they do, tension can still arise. In a successful marriage, partners are able to live with a certain amount of stress, and they do it by "letting some things pass." While it's true that ignoring or suppressing *all* angry feelings can create a hollow shell in which two indifferent "strangers" rattle through the motions of living together, it's just as harrowing if both partners are constantly lashing out at each other. For each one it's like living in front of a verbal firing squad, and though tempting, the immediate gratification of an angry return shot should be renounced in favor of a careful delayed reaction.

The Causes of Fighting

There is nothing mysterious about the sources of domestic strife. In fact, certain causes of marital discord can be easily predicted by outsiders who don't even know the couples involved. For example, one psychiatrist "predicted" coming events to the directors of a large investment firm by telling them as the Dow Jones average went down, marital strife in stock brokers' families would increase. Sure enough, it happened! The board of directors was so impressed that it hired the psychiatrist to come in and help relieve the very situations he had foreseen.

Some other causes of marital fighting are equally predictable. A worker is fired or laid off and his or her home life is rocked. Lack of money, too many children, lack of supports in the community, job insecurity—all increase the chances of conjugal conflict. When any or all these conditions exist, you can call on a friend or relative for aid or, most important, you and your partner can help each other. Put the brakes on bellicosity, sit down together, and tell each other you're in a tight squeeze. Don't say "It's your fault"—just pull together instead of apart. Sometimes, knowing *why* you're fighting is reason enough to be able to stop. Your knowing it won't instantly halt the squabbling but it will certainly help and taking whatever steps necessary to alleviate the situation *will* improve the marriage.

THE WAR BETWEEN THE SEXES

The current high level of anger between the sexes is a leading cause of fights external to the individual couple. It is so pervasive that it's hard to see. When marriage had clearly defined sex-role duties, there were fewer disputes and all things did not have to be negotiated. Today, men are literally mad at women for not taking care of them willingly and cheerfully the way their mothers did. One male psychiatric patient recalled longingly that his mother "did everything" for him—even ironed his underwear. Now his wife gives him short shrift, not starched shorts. His problem is not unique. Couples bicker over who does the cooking, cleaning, and baby-sitting because wives are doing more than cooking, cleaning, and babying their husbands.

Some wives are mad, too. They believe that their own mothers, if trained for nothing, are now unhappy in empty nests. Their mothers may have been bounded on the north by Proctor & Gamble and on the south by General Mills, but their daughters have expanded horizons. The Mrs. of today has learned a lesson from the servant-wife of yesteryear. She wants to be on equal ground with her husband, to develop and use her mind, and to earn money.

It seems to us that if gender no longer defines who does a particular chore like cooking or cleaning, some other identifiable, workable mechanism must be found to determine the division of labor or there will be chaos.

Unless a task becomes automatic, it can serve as a
never-ending source of argument and continuous day-to-
day negotiation. If the only criterion for who cooks on
Monday night is who feels like it, the opportunity for
haggling is increased. Sex-defined roles may be "out," but
rules of performance should be "in" and must be
established in the home. Negotiate *once*, and then,
according to each individual's needs, make rules. Until
that's done, there's bound to be a confused set-up in the
household. Husbands, angry at wives for not being just
like the girls who married dear old dads, and wives, angry
at husbands for trying to exploit them as their mothers
were, approach each other very, very cautiously. Neither
marital partner wants to be taken advantage of and each
is wary and stingy with the other. The agony of anxiety
keeps couples constantly on their guard and angry
because the partner doesn't give more. Partners in couples
like this must have confidence in each other in order to
create a successful marital ambiance together.

SPEAK UP—BUT DON'T SHOUT

When married partners approach each other with
cautious, reciprocal dropping of their guards, another
problem arises. Lower your defenses, take a chance and
put out for your spouse, and sooner or later you're
overtaken by the conscious or unconscious feeling you are
owed something back. If the implicit IOU isn't paid up,
you become angry, often without knowing why. This
feeling of debt can become a major underlying cause of
marital spats. People don't realize they are irritated
because they're anticipating something they're not
getting. Maybe they've worked hard all day or made a
wonderful dinner and now they want to be taken to the
movies, to be talked to, slept with . . . but the spouse just
takes what's offered and that's that. Many partners feel it
is immature to tell the other what is wanted and are
convinced it is more "grown up" to fight. They feel
embarrassed to go up to their spouses and say, "I worked

hard today and now you should hold me" or "I've been chopping vegetables for hours and now I want you to take me to the movies." Instead, they yell about anything, from money to in-laws. At the bottom of this vindictive compost is the earthy reason "I gave more than you and you don't recognize it or give anything back!" How much better each would feel if the other would make known what he or she wanted, didn't feel ashamed of the desires, and could ask for them without screaming.

ADOLESCENT MARITAL FIGHTS

Fights don't always arise from a disappointed reaction to openness. They can surface out of the wish to be less attached, confined, and dependent. You fear you rely too much on your spouse and unconsciously pick a fight to get a little breathing room: Now you can do more on your own! This device, a common ploy for couples, is similar to one used by most adolescents. Youth fights with parent in order to cut loose and become independent—indeed some young adults create a family furor just before moving out and establishing themselves on their own. A couple may drift into a state similar to that of teen-ager and parent, one in which the partners cannot allow each other independence, yet battle whenever together. It's like the teen-age girl without enough confidence to buy a dress on her own who takes her mother along, only to fight about the older woman's "taste."

Couples, like adolescents, often fight when they are unsure of themselves, perhaps to air hidden grievances. Anxiety has made it impossible for them to discuss subjects skillfully and calmly, so they resort to shouting. TV's "All in the Family" uses this device *ad infinitum*. Edith Bunker can only tell her husband Archie what she really thinks when she works herself up into a quivering rage, and then the revelation is usually about an entirely different matter.

If you and your spouse dislike going places alone, yet fight whenever you are together, or if you are afraid to bring matters up for discussion, then you have the adolescent's problem. You can combat it by enjoying brief *independent* activities and by "daring" to offer important subjects for discussion.

Adolescent fights are fairly common and more annoying than dangerous. They're an irritating source of wrangling, but usually not the cause of severe marital dispute. This "honor" falls to another category of combat—the childish marital fights.

CHILDISH MARITAL FIGHTS

The various psychiatric and psychological schools try, with different words and approaches, to get you to cope with the "child" in you, the little pocket of your personality that wants nothing more than to tapdance through life on the decks of the good ship *Lollypop*, the tyke in you who pouts and cutely stamps its foot when things go wrong. When should you feed this moppet within you? When should you ignore it, discipline it, make it grow? Childlike needs to be pampered, held, and cared for that are neglected by marital partners cause childish fights to arise. Everyone has these emotional longings and becomes angry when they are ignored for too long. All married couples fight when deeper wishes are not discerned and lovingly soothed. What varies greatly is how strong these psychological desires are and how forceful the anger is when not fulfilled. Much depends on our individual upbringing, whether or not our parents raised us with the proper balance between meeting our childlike needs and helping us to grow out of them and to learn to get what we want without becoming too angry.

Relying on one's partner to satisfy needs involves more emotional risk than working and keeping them under one's own control. By and large, even when you ask for it, you cannot be sure your spouse will hug and comfort you if you feel bad. People fight when spouses fail to attend to the child in them—fail to feed, hold, care for them. Sometimes they fight in a controlled, grown-up way even though motivated by youthful causes, but often the fight becomes loud, senseless, and babyish, achieving no goal and leaving both participants battered. If you find yourself so consistently irritated at your spouse that you cannot stand it, chances are you are relying more than you should on that person to solve your own life problems. Ah, but here's the rub! The more careful you are and *less* risk you take, the less emotional support, intimacy, contact, and good sex you get out of your marriage. In this case, you are more damned if you don't than if you do. It takes courage and strength to be open and remain on intimate terms with your partner because you risk frustration and anger which can turn to childish rage.

While there is no easy solution to the dilemma of when to feed and when to overcome the child in you, it is best neither to ignore the little devil entirely nor to cater to it exclusively. The former makes you a tough, sexless work machine; the latter puts excessive demands on your partner to treat you like a baby. One thing all marital partners should keep in mind is that people fight when they care more, so even if you do fight a fair amount, don't worry needlessly—it usually means you are emotionally involved and alive. Combats, however, should be of the *adult* kind, not the wasteful, enervating, adolescent-childish varieties.

Adult Fighting

Think for a moment about how much you and your spouse fight. A very few, the "saints," try to reach superhuman elevation and never get angry. A larger group, the "fallen angels," plummet to the depths of marital discord and always battle. The saints are unreal and unrealistic; the fallen angels are disappointed children—unable to achieve adult satisfaction; they blame each other for life's frustrations. In the thoughtless marital combat which we term "infantile," a hand-to-hand struggle for supremacy occurs, with little or no regard for the effect on the opponent or consequences to the relationship. Getting one's way becomes everything and there is no concern for how or when the battle is fought. Aggression is discharged with such wild abandon, the goal of victory becomes lost. Between saints and fallen angels lie the fortunate group we call "adults."

In adult fighting one partner never loses sight of the potentially damaging effects on the other person. Emotions are contained to prevent too much aggression from being expressed. If it is otherwise, the combatants know they'll be hurt and nothing will be resolved. Softening and restraining emotions does not mean denying them—it means making constructive use of them to help solve problems and attain a "goal." Adults watch out for the "same old fights," realizing that struggling repeatedly over who pays the bills or who takes out the garbage indicates they must quickly establish who is in charge of what once and for all. Occasionally, mature married partners have a battle in order to shake up a frozen, static situation. When one partner drinks too much, ignores household chores, or becomes sexually remote, the other may start a fight in order to be heard and to reverse the trend. Like other adult fights, the battle should move toward negotiation, not annihilation. It should result in a positive "checkmate."

COMING TO TERMS:
AGREEMENT, NOT VICTORY

Mature married couples understand that a "good" marital fight is really a "negotiation" in pugnacious disguise. To negotiate means to deal or bargain with another in order to reach *agreement*, while a fight is a vigorous striving for *victory*. Indeed, it would be better if we *could* call the mature marital fight an emotional, emphatic, and dramatic *negotiation*. Adult spouses know that winning is almost never important nor attainable in matrimonial disagreements; what counts is *accord*. Maybe it wasn't always so in the past or even now in all societies, but in modern America, one partner as consistent loser and the other as permanent victor doesn't work. For one thing, the perpetual loser becomes so resentful, that the union becomes unstable. In contemporary adult marital bouts, partners take turns in prevailing. After a battle over whose parents will be visited this Thanksgiving, there is no "victory"—just the knowledge that on the next holiday you'll be seeing the other family.

Learn to abandon the need to win and you have touched the essential point of adult marital spats. It's not easy for most of us who've been brought up to be competitive, to be fighters, to strive vigorously for what we want and to look down on losers. Furthermore, we are not used to noncompetitive relations with equals; after all, we've been raised to compete with our elders, juniors, and peers at home, in classrooms, on playing fields, and in offices. But the marital relationship goes beyond "win-lose" and works best when partners treat each other as noncompetitive equals. In marriage there can be no winner or loser...both must endure.

HONESTY—
NOT ALWAYS THE BEST POLICY

Victorians believed deception and artifice were essential to matrimony. Again, reacting to Victorianism, modern expressive psychologies advocated *complete, honest,* communication—a public broadcasting system of private thoughts with no regard for the listener. Believing in and beguiled by the Popsychos, spouses rushed to tell each other *everything*, including details of their love affairs. Husbands and wives said exactly what they thought of each others' looks, intelligence, manner, and behavior—often in public. One woman in therapy delighted in fixing her husband up with her own girl friends and then having a "rap session" to discuss his performance. "Diane finds him a good lover," she told the analyst, "but Alice agrees with me that he's a dead fish in bed." The wife shared opinions with analyst, friends, *and* husband.

Honesty of this sort is close to sadism in its self-centered disregard for the other person's feelings. No matter what the speakers' intent, it can cause vicious infantile fights when the hearers struggle to avoid the hurt inflicted by their partners. Sometimes, reacting against the "deceit" they feel they saw in their parents' marriage, spouses tell the Truth, the whole uncompromising Truth as a matter of principle, rather than intentionally to hurt. They must, they believe, steadfastly practice Total Honesty in their relationships. Blind, complete adherence to anything is foolish. The speed limit may say "40," but you'd better put on your brakes if children are playing in the street.

Even the Popsychos saw the light and finally recommended that couples ease off *full* disclosure, but by then honesty had become a religion. Partners they were treating indignantly refused to compromise and went on tearing each other apart! The center of marriage—trust, intimacy, love—cannot hold against such onslaughts to the ego. Men and women screaming the Truth should realize from their own reactions how awful it is—they must *shut up!* Containment is vital to contentment, especially in marriage. Emily Dickinson knew the value of restraint when she wrote:

> To fight aloud is very brave—
> But *gallanter*, I know
> Who charge within the bosom
> The Cavalry of Woe—

WHEN TO FIGHT

Realistically speaking, the "Cavalry of Woe" can stampede on occasion into an uncontrollable gallop and burst out of the personal corral. Whatever the cause, fighting is, after all, one of the primary methods of expressing distress for all animals. The American physiologist Walter B. Cannon noted long ago that an animal when threatened had either of two basic responses: fight or flight. For marital partners, the latter means divorce, so the former becomes practically a daily phenomenon caused by all kinds of injustices and disappointments. Fights occur over every one of the aspects of marriage—money, sex, leisure time, boredom, children, in-laws, career, power, and position. The bad feelings we all have at times are made easier when someone close seems responsible. Though it's unfair to the one falsely blamed, it provides solace and comfort to have a close person on whom you can dump angry frustrations. But, unlike Tom and Jerry, Road Runner and Coyote, Tweetie Pie and Sylvester, those cartoon characters who tear each other apart reel after reel and survive, we are not animated drawings, we cannot take a swipe at and tyrannize everyone around us with impunity; we have to practice the concept of *shutting up*. It's okay for Popeye to bat Olive Oyl in the teeth because she'll come bouncing back for more; but real couples must cope in less brutal ways. That's why it's a good idea to shut up until you are cool enough to have the "fight that won't go too far." While you can't *always* pick and choose the time to fight, any more than you can always do it calmly and rationally, the more you are able to decide dispassionately when to battle, the more often you will accomplish your ends. Don't wait too long and let the point of contention become stale and irrelevant.

Is This Fight Necessary?

It is reasonable to fight when you are trying to "change" an important part of your spouse's behavior which you've previously been unable to do through unemotional methods. Make sure the matter *is* important and that you are not entering the lists because you cannot accept imperfections. Fight when there is no other way to cope and only over essentials capable of quick resolution. This usually means some specific behavior that can be changed. For example, general arguments about "your mother" can be endless, whereas a struggle over some aspect, such as how many times a week you'll see her, can be settled. Hassling over a point which cannot be rapidly resolved allows a battle to go on forever.

Fighting becomes "necessary" because marriages are constantly coming apart or together, and when they are apart, the partners are not getting through to each other. A spouse may consciously or unconsciously resort to yelling and fighting to re-establish intimacy. The row can lower tense feelings of neglect and, in this sense, does clear the air. In fact, for some shy and distant couples, it may be the only way of making emotional contact for the moment.

HOW TO FIGHT

A classic Madison Square Garden boxing match is "arranged" and "timed." In a good NBA fight the champion is not placed in the ring with an unprepared, unwilling opponent but one who is warned and ready. To this extent, domestic fights should follow the ring example. In the household the combatants are their own promoters and timekeepers, and good timing requires each to discipline raw reactions. Such questions as "Will the fight achieve my ends? Is my opponent likely to get my message?" are worth asking before you leave your corner. Usually people hear better when not being attacked (it's hard to listen with a fist in your face). It may be very tempting to give in to the yell impulse and you might even feel good for the moment, but immediate gratification can lead to long-term consequences that are undesirable. By waiting for the "bell" or until you're not too angry, you'll be less likely to overattack and punch yourself out.

Round One

Boxing matches are meant to take place in front of an audience, but boxing couples should not. Those who fight in front of friends or strangers are either out of control or fear *losing* control in private. Outsiders guarantee that the struggle will not get out of hand, and for the fighters the witnesses represent "referees" ready to stop the contest if it gets too hot.

Round Two

When you and your partner live together, you know the other's weakness and may be sorely tempted to aim for it to deliver a stunning low blow. Do you really want to destroy your spouse? If you've married a dishrag, is wringing her limp going to help? Will throwing your husband's impotence in his face aid your situation? Even in disagreement, an intimate relationship implies an obligation to care for your partner's ego which has been entrusted to you. The worst violation is to stab the obvious vulnerability. You can end up winning a fight and losing a marriage. That's why when you are fighting it's important to stay on the subject and off each other's personalities. While it's fair to tell your husband you cannot stand the way he slurps over his soup, it's grossly unfair in an argument about table manners to toss in "Oh, and you've never satisfied me in bed!" That's mixing Emily Post with Masters and Johnson and it's *wrong wrong* WRONG!

Round Three

Couples should develop their own individual fighting rules as partners gain experience with one another. If A has a habit of stalking out of the room after a fight starts, which is the one thing B can't stand, B should take hold of A in a *rational* moment to get A to agree to stop going AWOL. If B throws things that come too close for comfort, A can discuss the "pitching" problem in a rational moment and get B to stop junking objects. Thus, the couple establishes the ground rules and limits for future battles.

In a fight, ask your partner for what you want specifically rather than telling him or her how to behave generally—you'll be in a better position to find a solution. Instead of a wife's shouting, "All you do on Sunday is watch football," it would be wiser for her to say, "Which game could you *not* watch so we can take a walk together?"

No marital battles should go beyond the Three-Round Limit and the partners should follow these "Marital Queensberry Rules":

1. *Forget the past.*

Fights should not dredge up what's gone before. Statements like "You always drink too much" or "You're always late" are attacks which lead to counterattacks and arguments incapable of solution. Fights should be present- and future-oriented. In the examples given, it would help to say "I would like you to limit yourself to two drinks tonight" or "I would appreciate it if you could be on time this evening." Your spouse can comply with such requests.

2. *Stick to the point.*

When your partner brings up a charge, it's not the time for you to counter with an entirely different allegation.

Answer your partner's charge and send *your* message on another occasion. Otherwise the battle becomes a free-for-all, a marital melee incapable of effective and rapid conclusion.

3. *Keep "So-and-So" out of it.*

"So-and-So wouldn't act like this!" is a standard cry in the matrimonial wail. When you fight, don't say or imply it would be better if you lived with someone else—the answer is too obvious, so keep "So-and-So" out of the picture.

4. *Watch out for histrionics.*

Everyone has a little Sarah Bernhardt in them and it will help immeasurably to learn each other's verbal tricks and emotional maneuvers. This knowledge will help you become less distracted, frightened, or fooled by your partner, and you'll be able to distinguish theatrical bombast from genuine anguish.

STOPPING THE FIGHT

When the manly art of boxing was in its infancy, the contestants simply went at each other until one of them dropped. Today there are rules about the length and number of rounds. Although the boxers don't know who will win, they do know when the bout will be over. Similarly, married couples need to have a sense that their battles will not go on forever. It makes it safe for them to have fights. The way to end a marital disagreement is for the contestants to know when it has gone on long enough and to resolve the specific problem at issue and/or to release tension through sex or humor.

A good fight can end with good sex. You don't have to wait until the relationship is back to perfect before resuming intimate relations. In some cultures, couples have sex first and make up afterward. We are not talking about the unfortunate, perverse few who can only copulate after a fight, but about partners for whom sex *can* be used to smooth over a marital spat and for whom it can do wonders for dissolving lingering bitterness.

Then too, there is the invaluable "sense of humor." Even in the thick of battle it can crop up and become a wonderful way to end a struggle. One woman could never get over the "funny look" her husband got after they'd been fighting for a while. "I get mad as hell at the s.o.b. and we fight. But his face turns red and his eyes start to cross. He begins tugging at his ear and starts to shuffle his feet ... *every* time we fight. Well, how can I stay angry at this guy who's turning purple and doing a St. Vitus dance? I try not to look but pretty soon I start laughing and then he starts laughing and before you know it the fight's over."

DON'T "RATHER BE RIGHT"

Nothing will ever be accomplished through fights if you don't learn that you cannot be *right* all the time. Even when you're sure your cause is just and you haven't won, know when a battle has gone far enough and stop it! To keep marriage fit, keep fits out of marriage. Realize that most of the anger coming your way is not really directed toward you at all. Life contains many frustrations making us lash out at our partners, but even as we do, we may harbor a tiny hope they will not rise to the bait. If they do, it's important to bring the matter to conclusion and not leave it a decisionless wrangle. There is no win or lose—TKOs and KOs are boxing-ring happenings not marital-fight ones. In marriage you look for a *draw*, with both sides gaining—one agrees to change, a secret thought is out, intimacy is re-established—whatever the outcome, the arm of both partners should be raised in triumph at the *end*.

CHILDREN

WHO THREW FASTER, Bob Feller, Sandy Koufax, or Nolan Ryan?"

The eleven-year-old boy is standing next to his father in front of the bathroom mirror and is using the older man's brush to arrange his hair in a pint-sized approximation of his dad's. The question continues a discussion which began two years before and shows no signs of waning. Even though Dad never saw Feller, scarcely remembers Koufax's speed, and has no sense of Ryan's fast ball, he doesn't say "I don't know"; instead he turns the conversation to Ebbets Field where Koufax pitched. They speak of the Brooklyn Dodgers, the Los Angeles Dodgers—on and on right down to the breakfast table where Jackie Robinson's astounding feats are washed down with Dad's second cup of coffee.

"There's a game on tonight!" the boy stands at the front door and yells to the departing car.

"Great, we'll watch it!" Dad calls out as he drives off down the street.

On Dad's birthday his son gives him a present: old baseball cards of Preacher Roe, Carl Furillo, Gil Hodges, Dixie Walker, and Duke Snider and reproductions of cards of Ty Cobb, Red Ruffing and Honus Wagner. The boy has toasted the facsimiles in the oven to give them the proper look of authenticity—Babe Ruth and Walter Johnson went up in smoke, but the remaining few are browned and beaten-up enough to pass for "antiques." Father and son look at the pictures and Dad holds up one with Ebbets Field in the background.

"Grandpa grew up near Ebbets Field," he observes.

"Yeah? Did Grandpa ever play baseball?"

"Yes, broke his nose playing catcher without a mask."

The boy is impressed. He finds it hard to picture gray-haired Grandpa crouched behind home plate. Talk turns to Grandpa's boyhood, then back to the old Dodgers. Dad tells the story of Ebbets Field, now a housing development with only the ghosts of baseball greats striding, sliding, and scoring down long, lino-leumed corridors. The boy realizes Fenway Park, *his* park, built in 1912, may someday too, disappear. Though they speak in the idiom of baseball, each understands the deeper significance. The son is finding out about the passage of time, the impermanence of ballplayers and ball parks and of life itself. In their talk of baseball, the generations meet, touch, and meld.

The department store fitting rooms are jammed with young girls and middle-aged women—each curtained cubicle contains a daughter working herself into the top, middle, or bottom of a garment. One preteener is struggling frantically into a pair of jeans. Even as she hops first on one foot, then the other, her eyes are always on the curtain edge making sure it does not part in the slightest from the wall. Beyond the "sealed" curtain stands the mother, arms full of possible purchases. She has been banished to the corridor, forbidden to look in and perhaps catch a glimpse of her daughter's unclad body. The woman is tired. She's been shopping all morning and longs to enter the tiny sanctuary and flop into the garment-laden chair. She cannot. Her duty is to run back and forth with clothing, to keep quiet unless spoken to, and above all to keep on her side of that curtain. To the right, another woman stands guard pushed into the same routine by her autocratic adolescent.

"*Mother!* Don't touch that curtain!!!" The sixteenth-of-an-inch border has been violated. With a sharp "whishhhh," the cloth is snapped and snuggled back into place. The mothers exchange glances. The second one sighs, "You have to be a saint." But even as the first woman smiles in agreement, her thoughts go back. She sees herself on the inside of the curtained room trying to slip into a bathing-suit top without taking off her newly acquired, scarcely necessary bra, glaring at the fabric-and-plywood frontier and commanding her mother to "stay out." Remembering this, she is no longer angry, not even tired. She feels at one with her daughter and with the memory of the woman who stood "outside" a generation ago. It is, she recognizes, a pattern.

These are two very ordinary scenes from parenthood. Usually dismissed, forgotten almost as quickly as they happen, they eventually add up and become part of a triumphant testament to the joy of having children. Rather than taking away from our lives, children add to them immeasurably—and by watching and teaching them, we ourselves learn how to grow up.

Growing Up and Liking It

When you have children, your life *isn't* over. You don't have to center your *whole* existence around suburban streets and PTA meetings; you don't *have* to become hopelessly child-oriented. Stay in the city, work, grow, use your mind, *and*, at the same time, enjoy a thrilling addition to your life. The media pendulum has swung from the Joys of Motherhood to the Joys of the Office, but you don't have to swing that far. You are free to have children and/or pursue a career. Do both if you like; or do neither. But don't be taken in by silly hype, by talk of the "baby trap," and try not to be influenced too much by slogans and political movements. As a matter of fact, to restore a sense of balance, make up your own counter slogans for fun...

> The Typewriter Trap
> The Filing Trap
> The Ringing-Telephone Trap
> The Meeting Trap

House *or* career work, both sides should keep their traps shut and let women "breathe."

If you think "work" means being a brilliant, sexy photographer or a zealous, noble social worker, while parenthood is depression and slavery, you are a victim of magazine writers who manufacture stories of the swinging career girl and the ardent do-gooder as opposed to the imprisoned housewife.

Remember this: It's not *where* you are but *who* you are; solutions do not come from the outside. If you are a lively career woman with a good brain, you will be just such a mother. Combine the two if you wish, but don't worry so much and don't read articles about the "decision to have a baby." Sure it's a scary and final decision—but deciding on a career is final and scary too! It's not just "play" being a "photographer," as those magazines suggest; there is a boss and deadlines and constant worry about whether you are above or below the standard of competence or just average. Being a grown-up is not just "playing"—it's playing for keeps, whether its having a career or having babies. If you have the interest and are willing to devote the time, children will add to your life; but if you have neither interest nor time, it's better to remain childless— for you, having children would be a chore and a painful mistake.

One thing is sure—being a parent does help you grow up, and maturity isn't a dull, frightening prison of harsh responsibility. You can still work, go to the movies, dance, have a good figure, be sexy, and possess a lively mind. A career doesn't give you all this and a baby won't take it away!

BEING A PARENT HELPS YOU GROW UP

When two people combine personalities and establish and guide the next generation in the form of their child, they become concerned for the living being they've created and cease being children themselves. Their own growth is accelerated. In fact, many couples don't seem to fully "mature" until they have children, or, at least, maturity is delayed if they don't have any. Thinking of someone other than yourselves, caring for a creature you and your spouse have created, taking interest in this developing person, delighting in helping and loving all give you a feeling of belonging, of strength, of attachment to the course of human history. When there are more than the two of you to consider, it can influence your standard of behavior for the better.

Sportswriter Roger Angell described exactly what we mean by this "increased standard of behavior." Baseball's Willie Stargell, a monumental slugger for the Pittsburgh Pirates, went into an "epochal slump" during the 1971 pennant playoffs and World Series. Up until the pennant race he had led his league in homers and played an important role in his team's affairs—indeed, he had propelled the Pirates into the final competition—but at season's end he plummeted from the heights right into the batting cellar. And yet Stargell endured repeated humiliations at bat with total composure, returning from home plate after strikeout or pop up "without the smallest gesture of distress or despair." After one of those "empty afternoons" Angell spoke to Willie in the locker room and asked the "proud intensely competitive man" how he "put up with that kind of disappointment without giving way to anger or explanation." Stargell gestured toward his four-year-old son Wilver, Jr., who was playing on the floor and said, "There's a time in life when a man has to decide if he's going to *be* a man." Roger Angell was unable to say whether he "most admired the principle or the philosopher's way of expounding it." We agree, the Hellenic, the noble, the *right* answer about the obligation of parenthood came from the heart of a real grown-up, left-fielder Willie Stargell.

The Real Truth About Children

The disadvantages of having children have been greatly exaggerated. There is no denying that disadvantages exist, but they are in fact temporary and far outweighed by the advantages. We will take up the major problems, try to show you how to minimize them, and remind you, that the sometimes tedious, often hard work of child rearing has ongoing pleasures and future rewards.

THE CHILD AS INTERRUPTION

A childless married couple has been compared to a pair of lovers on an extended affair. The concerns of each partner revolve around his or her own and the other's pleasures. The partners can have long, uninterrupted candlelit suppers or pick up at the drop of a hat to travel or visit friends. At home they can walk around naked without a thought and they can have sex in any room of the house. They don't get up to care for children and they don't lie down to sleep with worries about them.

The first infant rudely comes between these "lovers," husband and wife. Like faulty alarm systems, babies sound off, awakening parents at all hours with an incessant wail of want. Besides making hash out of sleep and serenity, babies also deprive father and mother of the ability to come and go as they please. Children are tiny thieves of time and the responsibility for a new life interferes with their parent's freedom in every way. The sanctity of evening and the sanctuary of home are attacked and assaulted by these miniature warriors and their persistent battle cries.

There is no question but that children meddle with a couple's time together, but the interruptions rapidly lessen as the newborn grows and learns to sleep through the night. Soon, the miracle of motor and intellectual development unfolds and parents are rewarded with smiles and recognition as the baby learns to feed itself and play with toys.

In child rearing, the mother bears most of the early brunt, but she has also experienced the joy of feeling life inside of her, of watching a child be born, perhaps of feeding it with the milk of her own body. There is physical pain in the act of giving birth and there is another kind of pain in early child rearing, a downturn in the curve of marital happiness. In each instance, the unpleasant is more than made up for by the developing new life you have created together. And there is a distinct advantage to be gained from the very "interruptions" of the newborn. Married partners are literally kept "on their toes"—they have to be flexible, creative, and open-minded, and this starts with answering the cradle cries. The narrow-minded can't be distracted from their focus of attention because they've never had to learn to adjust. If the couple with children risk exhaustion and loss of privacy, the childless one can become rigid and unyielding. As much as we may hate it at the moment, being interrupted is more good for us than bad. The bombardment of new stimuli keeps consciousness expanded; it makes you a happier person by getting you out of yourself, making you more adaptable. The more open to change you are, the better chance your marriage has of surviving the inevitable adjustments. If you want "clinical proof" of

this, a study at the University of Michigan found that
married couples having three children were more mature
and enjoyed richer lives than a sample of childless couples
of the same age.

THE INTRUDER BECOMES THE INCLUDED

Yes, the newborn arrives on the scene to interrupt
gourmet dinners, unhurried sex, lazy weekends, and
spontaneous nights out. The intrusions are resented, but
as people grow older they don't necessarily want to be
alone and are often glad of the presence of children. They
welcome conversation with them, enjoy taking them out
for an evening or on vacation. They treasure their
children's company for a variety of reasons.

CHILDREN KEEP YOU YOUNG

The responsibility felt by parents after children are born
makes the parents "grow up" fast and thus feel a little
"old"—but really, children eventually help keep you
young! They don't allow you to hang up your brains at the
end of a day but confront you with an endless flow of
questions, new ideas, and interests. Although the
generations occasionally become adamant with each
other, children's thoughts and enthusiasms alter the
outlook of elders just as parental wisdom and knowledge
strongly influence the young. Some mothers and fathers
make a point of reading and listening to what their kids
are "into"—Kurt Vonnegut, Jr., Carlos Castaneda, Stevie
Wonder, Elton John. Sometimes parents are enthusiastic,
other times critical. Perhaps it is not the norm, but
parents' ideas *can* be changed by their youngsters and it is
possible to "think" along with children while not "acting"
like them.

In so many ways, children draw parents actively into
changes in living styles. Many parents avow, for example,

had they to do it over again they *would* live together before marriage to test compatability. Also, children stimulate desires and interests which may have lain dormant in their parents for years. The sexuality of the adolescent can reawaken parental longings, even actions, and some prudish marrieds have become more lively and adventuresome in bed as a result of their offsprings' influence. Teen-agers' interest in reading, theater-going, and traveling can make parents consider and do the same. Every one of your senses is enriched as each brings new, sometimes jarring, often fascinating, stimuli to you.

As couples "relive" their own lives with their young, they stay close to their own feelings and enthusiasms. Each milestone of our children brings our own milestones back to mind—the first tooth, the first day of nursery school; learning to read, to ride a bike, to catch a ball; the first piano lesson, the dance, girl friend, boy friend—through all of these we touch our own pasts and become more human, understanding, and flexible in the present. The family is not a static, dull refuge, but a living institution animated by dynamic interaction between parents and children. It is a group in which all are changed—the young gain wisdom and the parents are brought up to date.

AND WHAT DOES ALL THIS COST?

Every once in a while an article appears in the newspaper about how it costs the average middle-class family over $100,000 per child by the time they've paid for music lessons, camp, clothes, the orthodontist, and college. This figure frightens young couples whose combined salaries barely seem able to cover their own food, clothing, shelter, and entertainment! They worry about the loss of some or all of the wife's income if she devotes herself to infant care or about moving to larger quarters when they can scarcely afford the ones they're in! It *is* true that children are expensive and do at times strain the budget, but they aren't nearly the burden the journalistic figures imply. Anything looked at *in toto* looms large. If you add up how much it costs to keep yourself supplied with cigarettes per year, for instance, you'd probably choke on your next puff. On a day-to-day basis, infants and small children really don't take up so much space; apartments may need be a little bigger but hardly mammoth. A woman's salary doesn't have to be lost if she wants to continue working, and as far as education goes, public schools are free and colleges are beginning to make scholarship arrangements for middle-class families.

Exaggerated costs frighten us, and in our fear we lose sight of an important point—children cost money but they're worth the expense! The middle-aged woman who takes a job to help put her son or daughter through college may complain, but she has something worthwhile to do, a purpose—the education of the young. In fact, though it seems she's complaining, she's actually proud and boasting a little. Similarly, popular "life-cycle" books talk about how upset middle-aged men feel when they reach a plateau in their careers and can't advance any higher. The popularizers forget that advancement isn't everything. Working for the benefit of children can give parents enough reason and purpose. In complaining moments, "working for the kids" may be depicted by parents as a burden, but in fact it's good for them. It's not a trap, it's a springboard!

CHILDREN—THE PAINS

At 11 P.M., just before the evening news telecast there's often this TV announcement: "It's eleven o'clock. Do you know where your children are?"—implying if you don't, they might be sniffing cocaine, stealing a car, or getting a venereal disease—in general, up to no good. We're watching out for our teen-age children because it wasn't too many years ago many people began to fear the adolescent and thus to stereotype him. Sadistic and sexual excesses were believed to be embodied in leather-jacketed, bra-less, amoral teen-agers; youth became a scapegoat. At present, some parents seem to almost blindly fear their own children. Not only can this destroy their pleasure in them—it can turn into a self-fulfilling prophecy in which impressionable youngsters, expected to misbehave, will. It is part of normal parental caring and quite natural to worry about children, but you will be less anxious if you look at them as they really are and not out of some exaggerated anxiety about crime and abandoned sex. Worrying about one's children is loving and human. Everyone agrees "involvement" is desirable, and when children are brought up in close, watchful, and loving families there is less reason to fear or expect them to do terrible acts before or after 11 P.M.

CHILDREN—THE PLEASURES

We live in a time in which negatives about having children have been overemphasized by the short-sighted whose motives are economic, political, and social. It is a historical fact that whenever money is tight and jobs scarce the birth rate goes down. More and more women want to work, and as the "working woman" is glorified, the "mother" is devalued. The stereotypic myth of the sexy, free, glamorous "career girl" is held up against trapped, depressed, dumpy "mom" and her brood. In their zeal, some zero-population-growth advocates and others deflate the joys of child rearing. All this is journalism, faddism, and nonsense. Here are the human facts. Children don't tie you down—they release your spirit. Youngsters don't make you old—they keep you young. The hurly-burly of their interruptions will not harm you or your marriage but will keep it fluid and alive. Their "expense" will give you something better to work for than just yourselves, and worry over them is part of the richness of human loving. Common sense dictates that your marriage and your life will be enriched by children.

Don't Let Children Split
You Up

Couples share responsibility for children, and if they manage well and keep the proper perspective, mother and father feel a sense of accomplishment and pleasure as they draw closer to one another. However, if the younger generation always holds stage center and the adults' needs are lost sight of, marital difficulty is inevitable. When infants are handled poorly, their incessant barrage of sound and demand is added to all the other drains of modern life, and Mom and Dad may indeed become very angry. His ears ringing, his mind whirling, husband withdraws and stays late at the office. The wife, upset at her husband's failure to help her with the noisy burden(s), may become depressed and may also withdraw from the home. Neither she nor her husband can face the mini-tyrant they're created. At worst, children represent yet another obligation, another instance when one has to give when one wishes to receive. That's when you should start thinking about your marriage.

THE ENERGY CRISIS

Children cannot be allowed to drain parents to the point where each of the exhausted pair tries to get the other to take over child care even though both of them are spent. If they do, the following unhappy but all-too-frequent scene develops. Husband returns from the city on the 5:50, drives home, and opens the door. Tired, beat, he wants a drink, a little relaxation, a little affection. Guess what he gets? He's greeted by a harassed woman, her throat raw from screaming at unruly kids. All she wants is his help with the children and a little affection for herself. Husband and wife wait for the other to give a kiss, bring a drink, care . . . in some way to attend. Neither initiates the needed action. Both stand angry and disappointed and each parent is left with the anguished thought, "It was never like this before the kids!" It doesn't ever have to be this way if the couple understands the problems and tries to work them out. The "tired" husband and wife should never get into the position of being washed-out, needy people waiting for the other to toss life preservers. Arrangements must be made to save a bit of yourself for each other. Most important, don't try to give the final drop of energy you don't have to the children and don't expect your partner to do it either.

MONEY, THE "FUEL" PROBLEM

Too many parents hide behind the excuse, "I can't do anything about it because it costs too much." It's true that a number of child-oriented solutions require money, but it's not a great deal and certainly little enough when you weigh the costs against the consequences. The simplest thing is to get a high school girl to take care of the children and give them dinner. When mother and father are both full-time career people, live-in help may be essential to prevent arguments over who is to stay home when young children are ill or need to be transported to a friend's house, a music lesson or the dentist. Either solution is a cheaper poultice to apply to baby wounds than a divorce, or a psychiatrist. If one sitter can't give enough time, use two or three or more; in fact, several are better since you'll have alternatives should one not be available. Setting up sitters will give you and your husband the opportunity to sit down, go out, enjoy each other's company, and talk over the news of the day.

When there is little money or help cannot be gotten, it is good to be near family. Willing grandparents can really help a *lot*. With Grandma or Grandpa in charge, you know the children are getting reliable, secure care and it usually doesn't cost anything.

There is really no reason not to have some assistance. Bringing up babies *with* help is not an elitist idea. Bringing up babies *without* help is a crazy one. With steady, proper coverage, the wife need not put all her energies into the kids, so she'll have something for her husband and not expect him to go "on duty" immediately in the nursery.

It is a law of human nature that everyone must get, so they can give. You and your spouse are not made of iron. Restore yourselves from the day and you will be able to turn to the children, not frantically but with patience. The threat to marital intimacy can be greatly eased through intelligent planning and recognizing the importance of private times and places even in a crowded home.

WATCH OUT FOR THE TEENS

When children are old enough to take care of themselves, there is a new way they can subtly monopolize time and hurt marriage. Teen-agers can cause battles in the home with and between parents. Boys fight with fathers over the car, household chores, and curfew hours, and daughters argue with mothers over clothes, dating, use of the kitchen, and straightening their rooms. Arguments range from the trivial to the significant, but it's not what they are about so much as the fact they exist and are exhausting and debilitating. Adults may get to the point where they feel they can never finish a sentence and are unable to get one another's undivided attention without a child interfering. Teen-type controversies can create bad feelings between husband and wife.

A lot of tension and trouble stems from parents' excessively high hopes for children, whom they may regard as little bundles of potential achievement. In their zeal to make sure their offspring are not lazy, live up to potential, do well in school, and in general do better than they, parents become obsessed with them. Too much attention is focused on the children and not enough on each other. It's time then to concentrate on changing the situation, and this is done through sensible childrearing techniques.

EXPERT CHILD REARING

Excellent books have been written on this subject but we would like to make a brief statement on the underlying principles, because it is so important to the peace and tranquillity at home and in marriage. Horrendous battles with children always adversely affect the marriage, either by inducing the partners to battle each other or by causing one, usually the husband, to withdraw from the unpleasant tension at home. It is noteworthy that techniques experts recommend in handling your children are similar to techniques used in a good marriage. Tact, diplomacy, and interpersonal skill are most effective—after all, children are people, and when treated badly, they will respond badly.

Good communication skills are desperately needed. Listen to your children carefully. It's fun to hear their ideas and certainly helps in dealing with them to know how they think. Concentrate not only on the words but also the context and hidden messages. Then indicate you've heard the request, and when stating your own views, especially when you disagree, don't criticize or name-call. The marital technique of constructive suggestion works equally well as a parental one. Say what you want but don't attack the person. "I want the clothes picked up off the floor," not "You are a slob." "I want you to do your homework now," not "You always leave things to the last minute." Don't express rage, but control and voice it in nondestructive ways. Sound familiar? Basically, it's what we've told you in the marital fight section: *shut up!* When you have cooled down, then try to re-establish effective communications which will produce a positive result. Attacks on others, spouse or child, lead to *counter*attacks and nothing more.

Realize also the need to steer a course between the two extremes of overprotection and indifference. The child must be helped to grow and exercise the responsibility appropriate to his or her age. To remain close as a family, you have to set up a dual-purpose household, one which encourages the young to leave while giving them enough closeness so they'll want to return. The trick is to help children gradually separate from you as they grow up, while retaining enough mutual respect and affection to prevent you from losing each other. You must not be too possessive. Guide, don't suffocate. (The possessive parent can really dominate an offspring's entire life. One such character was Maybelle Webb, mother of the late actor Clifton Webb. When she died in 1960 at ninety-plus years, Webb carried on like a madman and was inconsolable. "What's going to happen to me? What shall I do? Help me!!!" he sobbed to his friend Noel Coward. Coward fixed him with a stony glance and said, "Clifton, it's very difficult to work up sympathy for a seventy-year-old orphan." The web Mother Maybelle wove around her boy was particularly sticky, but the story illustrates how parents can overdo "holding onto" techniques.) Parents who support a child's efforts to separate will not be left in an empty-nested depression; they'll simply be a couple with an adult "child," enjoying each other's company, having a rich store of happy memories, and sharing many common interests.

Once you practice your child-rearing skills, try to increase your confidence in them. Some parents are so unsure of themselves, they retreat into a helpless form of fearful paralysis and turn entirely to experts, teachers, doctors, clergy, psychologists, psychiatrists, or the latest books to do their thinking for them. *Trust* yourself. Listen to your child carefully, be fair, do the best you can, and don't worry so much about making a mistake. Whether you do or don't let your children have the car, go to a dance, travel with a friend, or go away for the weekend will hardly make or break them or you.

Children as Causes of
Parental Dissension

Children of all ages are remarkably skillful in getting what they want from their parents. Sometimes it can be fun to watch the littlest ones scheme, but in their strenuous efforts to get their own way, children can cause dissension between parents—first, by manipulating one against the other and then by inadvertently causing them to disagree about child-rearing practices.

CHILD-REARING FIGHTS

Theories on how to handle infants always seem to be changing in the United States. Every generation a bevy of beliefs is trotted round and we go leaping to the latest conclusions. In the 1930s, for example, the inculcation of good habits was number one on the "good child" check list and training began in the cradle. The child had to get up at the right time, eat at the right time, and never ever be picked up when it cried. For fear of spoiling them, 1930s tots were allowed to wallow in their cribs. Then Dr. Benjamin Spock, echoing Sigmund Freud, decreed that the infant stage was crucial, so by the 1950s, parents had become permissive. If the little one was stymied in any way, it could be irrevocably harmed, they thought. Lasting scars would zigzag adult psyches. Neuroses would smolder and burst forth, and if things were really bad—look out! . . . schizophrenia! Believe it or not, mothers in the 1950s devoted themselves to their children in the hope of eliminating mental illness. American homes became miniature mental health clinics and were rightly described as "child-centered." Pediatricians guiding Grandma had told her regular meals, sleep, and play were essential and careful cleanliness vital. Grandma's grown-up little girl was told to guard against making her offspring into obsessive neurotics and to help them become creative, normal, and free. Thus, a mother could hardly use her own mother as an example of how to bring up an infant for fear of making her child rigid and neurotic. Grandma was hushed and shushed as Mom turned to the "experts," read books, and consulted doctors and radio programs, relying on them to show her the way. Now her children are grown and married and things are more confused than ever. The inculcation of regular habits didn't work and permissiveness contributed to pot smoking, dropping out, hippiness, and college riots. Just to eliminate any suspense over what *is* right, the current view seems to be *permissiveness about feelings and strictness about behavior*. The child can say he hates his parents, but he's not allowed to hit them. He's allowed to say he doesn't feel like getting up in the morning, even be sympathized with, but he must then get going.

NEED VERSUS HABIT

Parental disagreement in child-rearing practices, a factor from the infant's birth, usually increases as a source of strife as the child grows older. At first it's "Baby's crying! Should it be picked up?" The wife says, "He's hungry" or "She's in pain," while the husband says, "Leave him alone. Don't spoil her." These different reactions to the same situation illustrate the theory some experts call the *need* versus the *habit* in child rearing. If one regards the child as hungry or in pain, one caters to its need, but if one fears the "squealer" will learn to expect to be waited on as soon as it makes a peep, well, that's fostering bad habits.

As the child grows, the differences between parents escalate, creating dual parental upbringing philosophies.

These beliefs derive from what the individual parent really thinks about life, and different thoughts mean different ideas. For instance, a big question in any family is that of religion. Should the child receive religious training? How much? And if the parents differ, in which faith? Fundamental issues of why we are on earth are involved. Are we here for fun, for sacrifice, to work, to help others? Matters strongly felt by parents can lead to deep disagreements over a child's upbringing and often are unsolvable by compromise. A primary reason for this source of stress between American couples is the lack of consensus throughout our whole nation on how to raise children. Besides religion, dilemmas include such issues as strict versus permissive, competitive versus co-operative, family nudity versus modesty. In part, this ambivalence is due to rapid social change. Those parents wary of their own childhood experiences with their own mothers and fathers turn to experts for help. They feel they don't know how to act toward or in front of their children, because they had no good example to follow. A boy cries, his father calls him a "sissy," his mother insists he's sensitive. The difference in interpretation is nonnegotiable. Similarly, the question can arise about what time an adolescent girl should come home from a date. Dad says 10 P.M., Mom, 12 midnight. It is possible to compromise and get Cinderella home at 11 P.M., but if Mom and Dad firmly believe and are committed to their time stand, it can be impossible for them to reach agreement. A poor solution is for father to totally withdraw, leaving all child-raising questions to mother. A better way would be to develop an attitude in which one of the couple has the veto in case of a tie. This works better, in fact, in the child's early years. If Mother has primary responsibility for the infant's care it does not seem unreasonable for her wishes to predominate. These dilemmas need to be *worked out*, but should not provide an occasion for parental fights.

MANIPULATION: LITTLE WHEELER-DEALERS

Children, especially older ones, convert the marriage from a couple into a *group*. This doesn't have to be a problem, but it can be, especially when "pawns" force the "king" and the "queen" into wrong moves. Children are capable of manipulating parents with innate, consummate skill. The child goes from the mother to the father and back again in search of the answer it wishes to hear. Parents are played against one another like electronic dots bleeped back and forth across video screens. This can be destructive, for instance, if a child gets one parent to allow him to do something which infuriates the other parent. Strife then results between the marital partners, and the score against conjugal happiness adds up.

Manipulation, according to the dictionary, is skillful and artful management—in this instance, of people. We refer to a "manipulater" in a pejorative sense, implying not skill but sneakiness. We admire the former but not the latter, and this distinction must be observed with children. We don't mind their trying to get what they want so long as they use honorable methods.

Children can interfere between parents so as to hurt or help the spouses. It is hurtful when adolescents or young adults deliberatey divide mother and father just to get their own way. At other times, their interference can help the married pair a great deal even though it may cause momentary dissension. Suppose a man is careful with money and regards his wife as either too generous or irresponsible. If his children side with her and campaign for her to get a new dress or redo the living room, it can create "healthy" tension between Mom and Dad. Depending on the issues involved, the children's role, while creating temporary trouble, can be beneficial, especially when they act as go-betweens or help in bargaining sessions. When one spouse becomes too extreme, the partner bolstered by the rest of the family, can bring him or her back to reason. Of course, the danger inherent in using adolescents as abettors or arbitrators is obvious—couples must not rely too heavily on their offspring to modify and ease tensions between them or they'll be unable to deal with each other directly.

Finally, be aware of manipulation but don't fret about it. Rigid parents consult one another on every point before the smallest decision regarding a child is made, and to the child this seems as though one parent cannot make a decision alone; it also makes the child feel "ganged up" on. Expect childish hanky-panky because manipulation inevitably occurs from time to time, and when you fall victim, relax and laugh about it. You've been had this time, but you'll have another chance as long as you don't let it divide the two of you.

Defining the Roles of Parenthood

Think through your parental role and assign reasonable amounts of time to it so you won't feel guilty about neglecting your children nor angry at being monopolized by them. A comfortable amount of attention well paid will be a source of pleasure to you and your children.

MOTHERS

Mothers shouldn't stay home with children all day long and not have lives of their own, nor should they work seventy hours a week and ignore their children. Neither *selfless* nor *selfish*, a mother must strive for a balance in which both she and the child feel fulfilled and content as each gives to and gets from the other. It is bad for both parent and child if a mother feels taken advantage of by excessive, martyred giving to her child.

It's no surprise the happiest children have content parents. Unfortunately, at this stage in history, motherhood is sometimes regarded as a low-status, boring occupation with bad hours, no pay, and early retirement. Some women, who would otherwise enjoy watching and helping their youngsters grow, feel outside pressure to have a career. When asked, "What do you do?" they want to be able to say "I'm a lawyer . . . nurse . . . architect . . . doctor . . . writer . . . museum director . . . archeologist . . . psychologist . . . whatever"—never "mother."

By all means, have a career if you want to or need the extra money, but don't feel you must have one. For full-time mothers, establishing skills other than child rearing is a good idea, since you may want something to do when the youngsters go off to school and especially when they leave home. Working mothers must guard against having careers that demand such long hours that children and husbands are ignored.

Motherhood may not enlarge your bank account or give you high status at parties but the inner rewards are great. The bond between a loving, trusting, developing child and its mother is one of the deepest and purest in human relations. It may not provide the snappiest cocktail conversation, but it's a very interesting and rewarding way to spend your day. In fact, an observant, sensitive woman can tell wonderful stories about what the kids said or did, as well as what happened at the office. If some of the less human members of the corporate computerized world don't want to listen . . . it's their loss, not yours.

FATHERS

We would like to give men the same advice as women. If you want children, don't work seventy hours a week and ignore them. The excessively ambitious and aggressive pursuit of the status, pleasure, power, and money of a career hurts everyone—child, mother, and father himself. Abdicating fatherhood can lead to unhappiness and divorce. Why not enjoy it? The benefits are prodigious. Fatherhood is a delight. Helping and supporting your wife as you care for the children creates the shared activity that draws the marriage together. Tossing a ball with your son, helping him with homework, advising him—all this will remind you of your own childhood and keep you young. The love of daughters is like none other. Take time to savor it all.

Fathers have real "clout" in the home because in most cases they're away longer and are somewhat less familiar to the children than mothers. Dad's voice can carry more weight at times and he can take over for a beleaguered mother. This is especially helpful when young ones are tired and unruly.

In the course of household events, the father's support of the mother should not be too rigid. He should not, for example, become too upset when children express anger at Mom. Though it's normal for youngsters to get angry at mothers, fathers should see that it doesn't go too far. But if the mother is tired, irritable, unreasonable, and perhaps has been too severe, the child should have the right to defend himself. The same holds true if the father is the unreasonable one . . . the mother should intercede. This is one striking change from Victorian times we heartily support: children need no longer be seen and not heard. If they have been unjustly treated they have a right to say so, even occasionally to shout and curse. It must be remembered their emotional controls are not as well developed as the adults' and flare-ups are understandable and admissible.

A father should take the trouble to have a personal relationship alone with each child. Generally, Mom deals with children on a one-to-one basis and so indeed should Dad. Take them out for a walk, bike riding, to lunch, or to a ball game. Talk to them and get to know them. Listen to them! It's fun for you and its terribly important for them to feel they've known their father. When a man is truly a participating and loving part of the family, the marriage will be improved.

CHILDREN—THE JOYS

Take the time to open yourselves to the delights of your family. Men and women who overwork in careers not only can become exhausted and sexless with each other but risk a further hazard by missing the development of their children. In that sense, they become "childless." Their marriages deteriorate and they begin to feel they're staying together for the sake of the children, the same children they scarcely know. It would be wiser if they took the trouble to find pleasure in their children as well as in each other.

Children are one of the strongest ties holding marriages together, and having them makes us want to do and be better. It's a joint, pleasurable, interesting, challenging, and exciting task for parents to make thoughtful decisions about them. Through them we relive the joys of our own childhood and adolescence. Through them we are vividly exposed to social change and continue to grow ourselves. Watching these people the two of you have created grow and develop is exciting— truly a shared, mystical experience. Seeing, sensing each other in the physical and psychological resemblance of one's children binds a couple more closely together. The feeling of having roots and family is a deep comfort. You see your own parents, brothers, sisters in them. They provide a touch of the past and a promise of the future. You feel connected to the flow of life and have a sense of belonging.

MONEY

IN THE NINETEENTH century two outstanding thinkers investigated two fundamental areas of life involved in marriage. One of these men should be obvious—Dr. Sigmund Freud. The topic he explored was sex and he was surrounded by eager followers. The other man might not be as easily identified; his subject was less sensational and his disciples did not catch the public's eye. His name was Karl Marx and the topic he explored was economics. In the long run, the sexual revolution proved to be less threatening than the economic one, and in this country today Freud dominates. Though much of puritan America regarded both sex and money as "dirty"—things you washed your hands after doing or touching— virtually everyone now seems able, no matter how slowly and painfully, to make the transition from "sex-is-evil-and-to-be-tolerated-only-for-procreation" to "sex-is-good-and-an-expression-of-love-and-caring." Marx's subject, however, remains a "dismal science."

Even for Freudians, thinking about money was always a little dirty and anal, so economic explanations of people's motivation and behavior were down-played especially by psychoanalytic theory. The heroic standard of "nonmaterialism" waving over Freud's Vienna was picked up and carried overseas. Mutually satisfying, close personal relations seemed to be the answer to life's problems, not power and the distribution of wealth. Clinicians didn't like to view patients and clients in ignoble, unsympathetic terms, but along came the "social psychologists" and their notions of the "interpersonal market place." The idea that people relate to each other out of the abject desire to *get* something, rather than for such splendid reasons as the wish to achieve intimacy is anathema to the pure psychoanalytic soul, yet questions kept popping up. For instance, if closeness alone is the prime goal in a relationship, then why is an attractive woman or a rich man more desirable than a homely girl or a poor man? Why do we want to get close to the one and hightail it from the other? Freudians, perhaps naïvely, dismissed "beauty," and said the young woman's interest in the older man arose from the "oedipal complex," her wish to have her father to herself. Social psychologists countered by pointing out that *rich* older men are sought after while *poor* older men remain as alone as their youthful counterparts.

The disputes between the schools of thought continue, but in order to understand the impact of money on marriage we must call for a small psycho-socio-clinical armistice. We have acknowledged our debt to Dr. Freud, but it's about time we realized, like it or not, that Herr Marx was right—money *does* influence our lives...a lot!

Coming to Terms with Money

The Victorians neatly pigeonholed the three prime marital issues of sex, fights, and money by shoving the first two into the closet and bolting the door and leaving the third totally up to the man. *He* would support wife and children. *He* would manipulate family money—including hers. It was a Tarzan-and-Jane world of connubial finance. ("He provide essentials, She provide Boy and keep clean house in the trees.") So women were not to bother their pretty little heads about money. Victorian marriages just ignored the three no-no's, sex, fights, and money. In our time, the first two no-no's have moved onto center stage. Freud began the long process of bringing sex into the open in part by showing the ill effects of repressing it, and the "open expression" of anger especially in marriage has taken the country by storm. But money has only recently been spotlighted.

THE MONEY MUDDLE

Everyone knows money problems are a source of marital difficulty, but we don't know exactly why. We don't know how we *should* feel about money because there has been no fully accepted thinker on the subject and hence no ideology. Is money good or bad? How moral should we be about it? Should we tithe our income, share it with the unfortunate, save it for a rainy day, or spend it all on pleasure for tomorrow we may die? Why should we save for a rainy day when we have Social Security, a retirement plan, Medicare, and soon probably, national health insurance? Why, indeed? The basic confusion in the United States is widespread and far-reaching and for many Americans, unconscious. When that "mixed-up" individual gets married, the money muddle doubles. Psychologists and psychiatrists, uninterested for the most part in economic theory, usually do not fully comprehend the underlying cause behind marital money agonies. While we are aware of premarital sexual hang-ups leading to marital ones and are learning how to deal with them, it has somehow escaped the notice of most observers that premarital *financial* hang-ups can be just as devastating to marriage. Although the "classic" reasons for money struggles—the desire to hurt, control or rely on the spouse—can and do occur in marriage, the real cause is each person's total confusion about money *before* marriage.

THE CHILDISH VIEW

Charles Dickens' delightful philosopher Wilkins Micawber put it thus:

> "Annual income twenty pounds, annual expenditure nineteen nineteen six, result happiness. Annual income twenty pounds, annual expenditure twenty pounds ought and six, result misery. The blossom is blighted, the leaf is withered, the God of the day goes down upon the dreary scene, and—and, in short, you are forever floored."

It is a plain fact that childhood education about money leaves most adult Americans totally unprepared for its modern use and we are "forever floored" when it comes to finances. Children are brought up believing money is a finite substance to be used and put aside wisely. Ben Franklin, the patron saint of the penny-saved-and-earned, set down our cash credo two hundred years ago and we've been measuring up to it ever since. We teach our offspring the value of a penny, a nickel, a dime by giving them a regular allowance and requiring them to make ends meet, thus updating the Micawber monetary methods.

What little psychoanalytic theory on money exists is equally flawed and seems to have been formulated in the spirit of Dickens' character and to share his Victorian view. Orthodox theory tells us that attitudes toward money are set down in the early years, especially during the anal period. While Freudians say that the neurotic regards money as a possession to be hoarded, they don't say how "normals" should feel about money. (Undoubtedly, they favor "nickel-and-diming it" but they don't come out with it.)

And what of the wealthy? How do those that have it feel about what they've got? The rich don't care much for Freud, but follow Ben Franklin's monetary ideas and glorify a penny-ante philosophy. John D. Rockefeller gave away dimes, H.L. Hunt carried a paper-bag lunch to his office, and our current famous rich family, the Kennedys give their tots allowances and encourage paper routes. The children of the rich learn how to handle dimes and quarters but not necessarily how to manage adult sums. Most of us, rich and poor, deal with big dough by punching it down to manageable size, and though few of us have to convert nickels and dimes to millions, all of us have to make a transition from the Victorian child's view of money to the adult modern one. How then do you apply the "one-a-penny two-a-penny" philosophy to a credit-card world?

MONEY: THE EXCESSIVE VIEW

Sex and fights came out of the closet and money has come out of the piggy bank, but we're going overboard again. We simply don't handle our finances prudently in what the psychoanalyst would call an emotionally well-balanced manner. Encore, we are frontiersmen, eternally dissatisfied, boundless, even lustful in our wants. We ride our financial structure like a bucking bronco, only it's the rider not the horse who is ultimately broke(n) as we hang on to the saddle horn for dear life. We don't worry about paying now and trust our government will take care of us. The government provides money during periods of unemployment and in old age and soon it will probably provide complete medical care. The government is our tribal medicine man hopping up and down, shaking, rattling, and rolling and we are its stupefied willing patients. We are so benumbed by the federal fiscal sideshow that we don't stop to think that our "chief medicine man" sets a miserable monetary example and manages its funds worse than we do ours. It buys all the new military toys and doles out endless social benefits. We have become the land of the payment deferred and the home of the ever-growing national debt.

Of course it's easier to observe the pervasive disregard for a balanced budget in others. We get angry at our spouses so readily because we detect the credit-card mentality in them but we fail to recognize it in ourselves. Maybe our neighbors, parents, children, and spouses overdo, but so do we! Understanding your own money attitudes and behavior is the first and most important step in achieving financial sanity in your marriage. Don't for a minute think you are immune; almost all of us are caught up in the hot pursuit of the elusive good life and we are under barely perceived but constant pressure to conform.

THE LUST FOR MONEY
(AND WHAT IT CAN BUY)

Unlike bodily needs, desire for money is not limited by normal processes of satisfaction. We can only eat so much food and indulge in so much sex, but the appetite for money or the products it buys can be insatiable. Like Baucis and Philemon's ewer, we want our coffer ever filled. It's not the "high cost of living but the cost of high living" that traps us and we are literally compelled to spend. The catalyst, villain, and seducer is *advertising*, which forces open America's wallets, but advertisers need receptive audiences and that's us. Advertising offers the good life in the form of staples and luxuries, confusing us as to which is which. "Supersell" clouds our minds. Our eyes are covered by a nictitating membrane of acquisitive desire blinking up and down with cash-register persistency. We begin to believe we *need* everything we are shown. Television punches products at us and no blow is too low; even sex is dragged in. Subliminally, every woman watching sixty-second automobile commericals harbors the secret hope if she purchases a new car,

Ricardo Montalban or Sergio Franchi will pop out of the hood and grab her. And male viewers get the idea that if they drive those machines, they'll be magically transformed into Latin Lovers. In the old days, the movies whetted our appetites rather remotely for the good things but with in-home television, advertising impact has become monstrous.

"Reason Not the Need"

According to some theorists, advertised products can be broken down into three main categories: timesavers, pleasure givers, and prestige boosters. Timesavers are dishwashers, sewing machines, home appliances—anything designed to give us more leisure. Items to use for amusement include tennis rackets, sneakers, bicycles, golf clubs, boats, etc. Prestige objects include lavish art books, fine wines, antiques, automobiles—all of which can and often do single out the buyer as a person to be admired. The groups obviously overlap: a small boat can be used for fun while a yacht can give prestige.

We aren't always aware or may not like to admit it, but one of the reasons we want the finest money can buy is not just for quality but for status. In our mobile society, one can aspire and go higher but we need the accouterments, the signs of success, the shiny El Dorados and Cordovas, the palatial homes and expensive clothes. Realistically, status cannot be purchased; one's job or what one does give status. Money may be a measure of status, but *seeking* it is grubby and laughable. People swept up in the purchasing vortex have been fooled by the advertisers. Craving the finest, newest, most improved product, they spend more and more of their borrowed installment-plan money and go deeper into debt.

THE PURITAN ETHIC

Despite their willingness to spend, many Americans possess confused attitudes toward money. We have the lion's share of the world's wealth, but we still see money as bad, the love of it as "root of all evil." The upper classes are particularly skilled in practicing this ambiguity. Many New Englanders act as though money does not exist and never discuss how much something costs or what one earns. In their classic sociological study of New Haven, August B. Hollingshead and Fritz C. Redlich observed how much money it took for the established wealthy to maintain their standard of living without appearing as though they cared about money and the authors noted that the rich practiced a conscious reverse snobbism by looking down on "status seekers" as "Ugly Americans."

Conscious Reverse Snobbism: Brother, I Won't Spend a Dime

A psychoanalyst friend of ours from the Boston area has been driving a dilapidated old Dodge for years though he has enough money for any new car. When he complained for the thousandth time about his vehicle, we suggested (not innocently), "Why don't you get a small Cadillac?" "Are you crazy?" he answered. "I'd love to get one, but I couldn't drive a Caddy!" He couldn't. There are about three thousand psychoanalysts in the Boston area and probably none owns a Cadillac. Many an old Saab and faded Volkswagen, but no luxury car. Our friend will hold onto his wheezing junkpile until the last gasp of the exhaust pipe, putting up with all sorts of repair nonsense rather than trading in. He's a psychiatrist loaded with insight and doesn't recognize this is an example of status through nonpurchase. The funny thing is we could tell you the same story about our plumber! He's been driving an old Chevy for years and is always saying, "I sure would love a new car, maybe a Caddy or a Lincoln." "Buy it," we say. "Oh, I couldn't," is his answer. "If I ever came on the job in one of those cars my customers would say I was overcharging them to keep myself in fancy automobiles." Analyst, plumber, both have the same problem: they can't spend their money. They're part of the American mixed-up money scene.

Money and Marriage

When young people marry, financial fuzziness may settle in right away. The honeymoon is a perfect culture medium for growing future attitudes. The time-honored postceremony sojourn costs money, often a lot, and is usually paid for by parents, perhaps in cash, most likely on credit. Sprayed by Niagara's grandiose falls, browned by the southern sun—in whatever way bride and groom are hypnotized by the many and varied honeymoon havens, they get a taste of the good soft life which they may *not* be able to afford. Thus, the first break with childhood piggy-bank mentality is created. Maybe they can disassociate themselves from the fairy-tale fog of the honeymoon, make the transition back to the relentless glare of everyday, and return to a sensible pay-as-you-go way. Maybe.

Sooner or later, though, the good life's gonna get most of them, and they'll become converts almost without realizing it. About the time they start having children, they'll buy a home or redecorate an apartment. Whatever the surroundings, urban or rural, it will be something most can't easily afford. Next come the appliances, furnishings, clothes, cars, boats, prints, paintings—and soon they'll become modern Americans with big eyes and even bigger debts. The more they spend the more they must earn. Work hours are increased, extra jobs taken on. The partners soon have less and less time for each other. Closeness, companionship disappear as stresses arise. They don't "feel that way" about each other anymore. Realizing something is missing, they may decide to alter their frantic lives to deal with the impending estrangement. They will take a two-week vacation, get away from it all. Off they go—to Spain, Italy, France, or some hot little island in the sun. It's wonderful! But when they return, the debts (including the trip's costs) are even greater. Yes, they're a "team" again, but they've fallen further into the financial hole. Ironically, couples try to relieve their financial stress by spending even more.

Couples with adequate financial education *might* avoid these pitfalls, but not necessarily. When you're *committed* to deficit spending, knowing how to budget doesn't help. Look at our government. Each year an elaborate financial plan is drawn up by experts and yet the United States falls deeper into debt. This is the pervading example for fiscal responsibility, our economic ethos. No wonder we're confused.

THE MONEY TRAP

While we don't wish to take an excessively economic view of marriage—we are Marxist only of the Groucho order—we do see a striking and repeated pattern. The typical American, totally unprepared to face his own adult economic life intelligently, joins up with a similarly naïve partner. In the pursuit of happiness, in order to earn more and more money, the two repress their own natural sensuous needs both individually and collectively. Love and companionship yield to the cold discipline of the work place as they struggle to support a very expensive addiction, the cost of high living. There is no hereafter, so buy now.

Caught in a slough of dollars and sex, the modern American couple tries to pull itself out and become sexually and financially unrepressed. Initially, the sexual problems can be eased, but as the couple goes deeper into the financial hole, sexual activity suffers too. You cannot exhaust yourself in money pursuits and expect to keep up with your sexual ones. The pressure on married partners is toughest between the ages of thirty and fifty. An American couple is in the most serious debt during these decades and worries more over money and making ends meet than anything else. The cause of its woes is the residual buildup of earlier days, both the premarital monetary helplessness and the subsequent desire for an endless "honeymoon." At this stage, the dollar shortage can either help pull husband and wife together or drive them irrevocably apart.

MONEY TALKS

The symbolic meaning of money is determined by parents, peers, life experiences, and mass media. The way a couple uses money serves as a convenient screen onto which fears, moods, aspirations, and attitudes are projected. Husband and wife can, and often do, have completely different attitudes toward money and project incompatible images. One may have been raised to regard money as a form of security: pay as you go and save for tomorrow. The other may come from a home where money was regarded as a necessary means to enjoy life. When "pay-save" marries "charge-spend," the offspring is conjugal discord. Because of differing attitudes, some couples try to avoid the subject of finances, but like the disinclination to discuss sex, the inability to discourse on money is bad for marriage. Money requires even more ongoing delicate negotiation. If you are deeply convinced you should not talk about finances in your polite, marital society, you may end up in a matrimonial mess with no idea why. However, if you keep your eyes open, there are "signposts" all along the way.

THE SCAPEGOAT SYNDROME:
PROJECTION AND PROFLIGACY

Mixed attitudes about money exist in all of us, and marital troubles occur when one partner, assuming all the positive feelings, attributes all the negative ones to the spouse. It works something like this: The Freudian notion that money is dirty and bad comes over us, and though we want as much as we can get, we're guilty about our lust for it. For example, a doctor decides he needs a lot of money because of his wife. *She* has social aspirations, *she* is always entertaining, *she* needs clothes, furs, jewels. He is the pure one, the Scientist; she is the profligate. The good doctor may in fact unconsciously encourage his wife to spend excessively to justify his pursuit of the dollar, and when those pangs of guilt about his own behavior assail him, he can yell at her. It really is a form of scapegoating in which all unattractive traits are seen in the partner, who must be punished for them.

Projecting your own feelings of guilt onto your partner and then fighting over it is only one consequence of believing that money's bad. A couple may unconsciously conspire to get rid of the bad substance and squander it. By this method the partners keep themselves perpetually broke and in debt and can have knock-down, drag-out fights over who's at fault.

Projector and profligate are two of the unconscious, polarized roles assumed or assigned by marital partners. There are others. One can be the Irresponsible Child, the other, the Cautious Adult. Child-Wife gets an allowance and Daddy-Husband chastises her for wasting it. Maybe she's really a shrewd woman but prefers to assume this advantageous pose in marriage. Even if she is a bona fide baby, the marital situation solidifies her infantile position instead of helping her grow out of it. Or the wife can be the "managerial" type to whom husband gives his pay check for her to dole out. Depending on how she handles the funds, the managerial woman can be good or bad, and that brings up an important point. We believe, whatever the future of marriage as an institution, a woman's financial role must be that of absolute equal. She must understand stocks, bonds, investing, banking, accounting, income tax, record keeping; health, life, fire, and property insurance; wills, estates, and legal matters—and be prepared to manage if she has to. If she feels inadequate, there are courses, either privately or university affiliated, dealing in finance that are offered specifically for women.

OPPOSITE MONEY MATES

The miser and the spendthrift often share one roof. Like Jack Sprat and his wife, they are incompatibly compatible. Neither can live without the other, but that doesn't prevent them from complaining. In most cases, the husband is the "miser" and wife performs a service for him he cannot do himself...spend. She gets him the good things of life, the extras, the doodads, while he keeps her financially solvent. It's a good example of polarization. Single, she would be forced to assume complete financial responsibility for herself, while he would have to break down and buy the good things he craves. In that sense, each would have to be more adult and admit personal accountability. With a spouse, as we've noted, you can project what you consider the less desirable onto the other, "My husband is the stingiest guy in the world ...My husband is so tight..." "My wife doesn't know the value of a dollar...My wife spends money like it's going out of style..." The needle is stuck in these grooves and the marriage goes whirling around. Eventually it becomes a power struggle. If you're too thrifty, learn to spend, and if too careless, learn to take responsibility.

MONEY, THE GREAT MANIPULATOR

Some husbands manipulate their wives *through* money, while women sometimes do the same to their husbands *for* money. In the battle for power, men are armed with funds and women gird themselves with sex; money and sex are both powerful weapons. A girl learns from Daddy early on how to bat her eyes and get what she wants. In marriage she uses "charm" in the same way. For men, money represents power and virility, and, if you recall, Mae West put it all together in her famous remark to an admirer, "Is that a roll of hundreds in your pocket or are you really glad to see me?" A husband may hold back money when he is not satisfied, but that doesn't mean he's necessarily a miser. The true miser is a rare bird, but the stingy husband is all too common. This man doesn't worship the dollar, but uses it for his own purposes. He is either selfish and wants everything for himself or withholds funds from his wife to manipulate her behavior. Maybe he's angry at her because he's not getting what he feels is his rightful quota of sex, love, meals, or companionship. On the other side, the spendthrift wife may be acting hostilely because she wants to get something she's not getting out of the marriage and feels constantly shortchanged.

Fortunately, this old system is well into its decline, partly because more women work. In fact, one reason some wives are reluctant to stop work and have babies is fear of having to ask their husbands for money. Such fears are not unfounded. It is wrong to try to control marriage partners through money. They will hate you for it. People do not like being forced, and the best solution is not "mutual manipulation," but rather family resources being shared and divided equally.

MONEY AS A SUBSTITUTE

Money can also be offered as a crisp substitute for love. Busy, well-to-do men buy expensive presents for wives they rarely see and allow their women to spend lavishly. The tacit understanding is that unlimited funds are taking the place of personal attention. In distant, businesslike marriages, the partner is either bought off or the couple confines "intimacy" to the money session. Couples who rarely sleep together will go into a huddle once a week and carefully pore over the budget. These monetary marital arrangements can succeed when each person goes along with the status quo. But in most cases money is no substitute for love. The individual feels hurt and neglected, and as warmth and contact move out, fights move in. Husband yells at wife for "wasteful practices" when he really wants to cry for closeness, attention, and perhaps sex. He resents her ingratitude—see how well he supports her! He doesn't realize that he's made her an offer she couldn't refuse (unlimited funds) but that the bribe isn't working. She feels he gives her presents instead of himself. Money is no substitute for love.

The Balanced View

Handling money requires more co-operation than achieving mutually satisfying orgasm. In sex the partner's needs can be taken into account for a few hours a week, but money demands steady attention. You should rate a spouse's financial co-operation in the same way you do your partner's sexual co-operation as follows: Does your partner deal poorly or well with funds? Does he or she spend too much or a reasonable amount on clothes, entertainment, cars, gadgets, or drink? Does your partner ignore or consult you about major purchases? Does he or she balance the checkbook incorrectly or correctly? The answers to all these and more create the atmosphere for the financial family co-op. If you recognized a lack of co-operation in your partner, try the harder questions. Ask *yourself*, "Do *I* spend too much money without regard to over-all financial requirements?" If the answer is "Yes" and the excuse is "I do because my spouse does," then the way to begin to improve the situation is to start with *you*, not your partner. Each of you going your economic way puts an incredible strain on your marriage and one of you must take action. Don't wait to be led.

THE FAMILY CO-OP

Sit down together for a talk and have last year's figures in front of you. See how much went for necessities and luxuries and don't come on too strong if too much went because your partner was extravagant. Drop the accusatory tone and use the same approach you would in trying to *improve* any situation. Berating your partner for wasting money will get you about as far as yelling at him or her for being impotent or frigid. "Co-operation" implies the wish to give the other pleasure while taking enjoyment for oneself. You have to decide together what can be spent and for the benefit of which partner. Remember, it's important to bring a spirit of generosity into the co-operative procedure. With modifications, your text could be O. Henry's Christmas story "The Gift of the Magi," in which, unbeknownst to each other, a husband sells his gold watch to buy his wife an expensive comb for her beautiful hair while she cuts and sells her hair to buy him a chain for his watch. Each partner gives all he or she can for the other. On Christmas Eve they exchange presents, on the surface now useless, but in fact very deep measures of their love for each other. Yes, it's a bit corny, but the concept is quite applicable. If you and your partner both want something *now* you must compromise if you cannot afford both. Let one make the purchase and the other wait—or could you both wait till your savings are expanded? In the end, you'll each get what you want and have a better sense of working together as a team.

MUTUAL ALLOCATION

Until recently, most married couples used a "pooling" system for money. Whatever they had or earned went into a general fund. Now, however, a new method commonly used where both partners work has evolved. This "Bankamerihome" system maintains strict separateness of the wife's and husband's money. The wife buys what she wants when she can afford it and the husband does the same; neither exploits the other. The system allows for the joint purchase of commonly used items, such as TV sets, refrigerators, or furniture... but, there's a madness in this method too. Unless the couple co-operates in the spirit of generosity, it can deteriorate into an exacting division of nickels and dimes, with each watching the other like two children doling out peanuts from a jar (one for you, one for me). And jealousy can be aroused when one makes a lot more than the other and has a larger store of "nuts." Also, if strict separateness means not having to consult the partner, this can turn them into "married splits."

If each of you are equal partners in the business of marriage and have equal right to determine what goes on financially, whether you have separate or pooled accounting, there will be many fewer battles over money. You can achieve this by trying to use funds as a team rather than against each other. Take turns buying and *always* consult on the purchase of big items. And don't be afraid to enjoy your money. Once in a while, it's okay not to be too serious and adult and "play" with dough. Some couples have a "madcap fund" in which they deposit a certain amount to spend solely on pleasure. If your funds are low, set a limit and you know you can spend up to the specific amount and no more—but within that range, have fun. Help each other recognize money hang-ups involving status seeking, dependency, or attention getting. Instead of pointing them out sarcastically, give your partner the boost or attention he or she is obviously looking for.

Husband and wife must practice mutual responsibility, the reward will be security and dignity. Neither partner should take the childish attitude that money "makes me nervous so you handle it." Neither should feel controlled by the other. Each has a right to expect generosity. Result, as Mr. Micawber would say ... happiness.

CAREERS

How MANY REFERENCES do you hear to "dual jobs" or "dual work"? None! It's always "dual careers," because a "career" implies a moral or intellectual endeavor undertaken for more than money. We plug along at a job, but we seek and reap the rewards of a career. Though there are more and more matrimonial dualists, the majority of marriages still reflect the old-fashioned union in which man as provider leaves the house in the morning and returns in the evening. He may return with tales of monotony, woe, and pain on his lips, but what happens to him in between those hours is not necessarily the torment described. Consider the case history of one such "breadwinner," Sam Owens. His profession is rather special but his problems were quite typical.

Play It Again, Sam

For eleven years Sam Owens played in the viola section of a large city symphony orchestra. While not really distinguished, his musical career provided a steady income, enough to keep him, his attractive wife Anita, and their three children in split-level, two-car comfort. Year in and year out, Sam trudged to rehearsals, appeared in performances, gave a few lessons, and went home to his wife and kids—until the regularity finally got to him. Frustrated and depressed by his work (he had failed an audition for a front chair in his section), Sam decided to do something about his life. He began to study conducting. After five years he was good enough to pick up side jobs with small ensembles in and around the city, sometimes straight symphonic work, other times with ballet or opera companies. Little by little his reputation grew and he was asked to conduct in other states, even way across the country. But all this was in addition to his regular symphony job, and time became a problem. He was home less and less and his absence troubled Anita more and more. Her husband was no longer around to help bring up the kids or keep her company, and when he did return, he was so exhausted from his new career he barely spoke, opting instead for TV and a drink. Anita began to nag—about his drinking, TV watching, lack of conversation, and long use of the telephone to set up conducting dates. Lonely and upset when her husband was away, Anita acted like a shrew when he was there.

At the same time his home life was stagnating, Sam's career was moving forward. The men and women in the orchestras he conducted were thrilled to learn from him and called him "maestro." Audiences liked his conducting and his pleasing personality. The ladies circled around him, paying appreciative, worshipful homage, and invited him to fancy suppers and parties. He went, most often without Anita. On his regular big-city job Sam Owens was a last-string nonentity; in his other role as itinerant conductor he was a demigod, a major minor-league talent.

"ZING" WENT THE STRINGS...

Inevitably, the new career brought him in contact with female performers...attractive ones. They vied to catch his eye because he could help their careers. One young woman, a solo violinist, was especially appealing. Fifteen years younger than he, she thought Sam very wise and charming and she eagerly sought his advice. In due time, he became her mentor.

Now Sam had a choice: he could either spend his time with an admiring, talented, beautiful younger woman who "understood" him or go home to a tired, angry, depressed, critical representative of his responsibility and middle age. The younger woman considered him brilliant, the older regarded him as a "shirker." Worse, he continued to act dull around his wife. Happy hours were spent opening his protégée's eyes to the wonders of music and the world, but his wife got only sleepy, silent, sloppy seconds. Anita became angry and sexually cold, and by doing so she reinforced Sam's desire to stay away, which he did.

VARIATIONS ON AN EXTRAMARITAL THEME

The old cliché "So-and-So is married to his job" does not describe this situation quite correctly. Sam Owens was not married to his work—he was having an affair with it. In pursuit of a career, he was sought after and admired. He appeared at his best because it provided him with an escape from the daily drudgery of his life...his marriage.

Sam Owens was sharp at work and flat at home. To be all charm and grace at one and all spent and blah at the other poses a grave threat to marriage. If home is nothing more than an aluminum-sided womb into which an exhausted career person flops, fuels up, and leaves, then the partner cannot help but become hysterical. The Owens marriage was okay as long as Sam stayed in his place, helped with the kids, and occasionally took out his wife. But once his ambition was liberated and accelerated, he became completely caught up in being Somebody, and the little time he spent at home became detrimental to the marriage.

Because of his career, Sam removed himself from the world of his marriage and Anita could not meet the challenge of holding on to him. As Sam withdrew, Anita grew morose and angry, having few resources to cope with her loss. The Owenses separated and eventually divorced.

THE COMMON CAUSE

In modern America the middle-class family often becomes isolated from kin and lifelong friends. Heavy expectations are therefore focused on the marital relationship to satisfy *all* social, emotional, sexual, and intellectual needs. The returning husband is the center of the universe, and if he strays, the wife is left companionless. A husband's career often comes between couples and causes tremendous strain. The question is, why would anyone prefer work to home?

The Secret Pleasures of Work

Work presents an outside challenge to marriage and is the one activity couples do not do together. All other areas we have considered—boredom, leisure, sex, fights, children, and money—have the potential to be dealt with by husband and wife as a pair, but in most cases, work must be performed away from one's spouse. It then becomes a *legitimate source of separate gratification*. Everybody wants to be part of a good thing, and if the nonworking spouse thinks the partner is having too good a time at work (*away* from home), jealousy, suspicion, and "me-tooism" take over. In part, that's why the enjoyment of work is often hidden from the marital partner behind a barrage of beefs as the career person poor-mouths his pursuits. The lyrics, while hardly Cole Porter, are very familiar: "I'm working too damn hard!... The meetings are so dull!... The boss is so demanding!... I'm worried the contract won't be signed!... I couldn't sleep all night, I was so worried about business!... I'm afraid the customer is going elsewhere!... Oh God, business is awful!... What am I slaving away for?... All that work for such little money!... I'm absolutely bushed!!!" These common concerns or expressions of fatigue and dissatisfaction may also be conscious or unconscious attempts to disguise what can be the *pleasure*, the *supreme pleasure* of work. Surely, the satisfactions derived from doing his conducting job well were greater than those from any other activity Sam Owens was engaged in, including his marriage, but he never said so to Anita. He just talked about how tired he was, how overworked. Sam was hedging and hiding the truth from his wife by emphasizing the "exhaustion," not the exhilaration of his career. It's a technique that comes naturally to many working spouses.

AND WHAT DO YOU DO?

Human beings are goal-oriented animals, and work provides a structure, an armature of prescribed activity for their efforts to achieve their goals. Need for money forces them to the place of labor where definite daily duties must be done, and the people with whom they toil constitute a social organization which can become more important than the activity itself. People who work together care about each other, become close, and form friendships. This is one reason why retirement for many is a trauma.

But the pleasures of work are more than just social. Opportunity is given to *define* yourself. I am . . . a baseball player, locksmith, airplane pilot, stock broker, cab driver, watchmaker, etc. In our society, those who don't work have a hard time saying who they are. We ask, "What do you do?" and are stopped short if the answer is "Nothing." How can you size up someone who doesn't *do* anything? An unemployed American is a misfit.

YOU ARE WHAT YOU DO

Once defined by our work, we're on the right track to satisfy different desires. More money can be made to buy the things needed for the good life. Thus a method exists to realize ambition, to gain power over others, and to shape events. A person is defined by his work and so is his status. The leader gets his way and can make decisions, often important ones. The Ivy League professor of economics is called upon for consultation by giant corporations, the New York *Times*, the President of the United States, while the high school teacher of the same subject settles for less. The more important the job, the more money it pays, the higher the status, and the greater the feeling of self-worth it confers. Many psychiatrists emphasize how self-esteem comes from within . . . ah yes, but *outside* recognition on the job can sure boost the ego too. Getting a fat raise or a promotion or being made a partner makes the recipient feel wise, appreciated, and self-confident.

Sam Owens' conducting career gave him a feeling of taking part in the affairs of the city, the country, the world, as no home activity could, and it became a pleasure. Of course, his career was unique—not many wage earners are maestros and even fewer can turn themselves into vest pocket Leonard Bernsteins. But all men are faced with the problem of work versus pleasure and would like to find, as Sam did, the latter in the former.

PAINTING A DISMAL PICTURE

The secret pleasures of work are not recognized by most people. Mark Twain neatly captured the common view that work and pleasure are antithetical when he observed in *The Adventures of Tom Sawyer*, "Work consists of whatever a body is obliged to do and play consists of whatever a body is not obliged to do." Twain applied this twinkling hypothesis to one of the most famous scenes in American literature, the whitewashing of a fence. Faced with the horror of hours of work, young Tom pretends it's a great pleasure. Soon his cronies are begging for a chance to help, but Tom pretends not to want to "share" his pleasure. Finally he breaks down and gives them a chance. Lo, the job is finished with scarcely a swipe applied by Master Sawyer. By playing up the delight, Tom made a laborious task seem desirable.

Long before Tom Sawyer, men discovered it was equally wise to *reverse* the procedure, to play down the pleasures of the outside job and emphasize its difficulty and unpleasantness, and they continue to do this today. Instead of whitewashing work, they painted it in dull hues. The effect is twofold: (1) It enables them to get more service from their women once they come home. After all, isn't it a wife's duty to care for the poor guy slaving at work all day to support her and the kids! (Sure it is! Get the slippers and pipe—here comes the guy who's suffered, and you *know* he's suffered because it's the first thing he tells you!) (2) It also keeps secret the pleasure attained *away* from the marriage. (The "miserable" job could easily consist of stimulating work hours plus a leisurely lunch, a game of squash or a round of golf.) The down-playing also minimizes jealousy in the wife and permits the man to stay away longer without being questioned. The career takes up outside time, and the worker finds it easier to say, "There is somewhere I *must* be," rather than "There's somewhere I'd *like* to be." While nonwork-related activities may make a partner feel there is someone or something with whom or which her spouse would prefer to spend time, the excuses "I have to work late" or "I have to go on a business trip" are nonnegotiable and nonthreatening.

The Career Trap

In order to live the good life, enough money must be earned to keep up. The worker "traps" himself into economic necessity by ever-increasing material desires, but a career is really more than money. No matter how people emphasize the monetary aspect, they admit, by a whopping 90 per cent, when skillfully questioned, that they would work even if they had independent incomes! The pleasures of work are indeed much greater than the pains, and couples must watch out for work's trap. The excessive pursuit of the dollar, the irresistible lure of status and accomplishment, and the preoccupying friendships on the job are piranhas of power which can chew marriage to bits. Unfortunately, the system rewards the fanatic—the man out on the campaign trail every day for two years wins the election, and the employee on the job earliest and latest wins the promotion. But watch out—your success can be hollow if you lose your home and family.

WORK AS AN EXCUSE FOR SOCIAL LIFE

American men do not have cafés or bistros where they can go to talk, drink, eat, write letters, or read newspapers. Even attendance at men's clubs, union meetings, and bars is significantly down these days. Men are with their wives or they're working. In order to create some sort of life apart from home, they welcome business opportunities to socialize. In most cases, it's not a conscious ruse to get away—often they have little control over it and the boss may indeed suggest they take a client to dinner or a show.

Work thus both provides and legitimizes a social life apart from the spouse. In many respects, getting away from the partner has been institutionalized and made part of the job. Wives used to complain about husbands going off to the neighborhood tavern or down to the gym or just over to the corner with the boys. They nagged, but it was expected behavior and there were compensations to be found in children, family, friends. Now the wives complain about husbands going off to work, but there is less they can do about this because there is the overwhelming possibility their men *have* to be away.

THE TIRED MAN
AND THE EXPECTANT WOMAN

The kinds of jobs or daily activities men and women have affect what they want at the end of the day. The "tired" man may have spent eight hours or more talking with his peers and not want to talk very much to his wife or anyone. The housewife, dealing all day only with children, may at the same time be eagerly anticipating her husband's return because he's the first adult that day with whom she'll have significant contact. So she's ready to chatter while he's ready to clam up. Depending upon how each has spent the day, there may be more than conversational stresses encompassing active-passive, so-cial-solitary, or indoor-outdoor activities. The hours spent away from each other siphon off an incredible amount of energy from both parties, and how they greet each other now and what they do together must be worked out and not left to chance.

All careers demand time but there are different levels of commitment, and a wise spouse learns to distinguish between being permanently ignored and being temporar-ily neglected. A legitimate need requires an understanding partner, and it's absolutely essential in marriage to make allowances for career stages. Any young person starting out in a demanding profession is called upon to overwork. A doctor completing his training and "moonlighting" to start a private practice may work an eighty- or ninety-hour week for up to two years. A spouse who panics at this absenteeism from home adds extra stress to an already overworked partner. It would be better to be patient with the doctor, at least till he establishes himself, and not hound him. It's easy for us to say "be patient," but it's difficult for a spouse to figure out whether her partner will ever stop overworking and how long patience will be necessary. Some men ease off, others don't, and it's not that simple to predict which ones are which. There are people who make a career out of being busy and a spouse should learn to read their signals.

It's oh-so-tempting to be overzealous on the job, but if you ignore your spouse for your career, the ubiquitous vicious circle is set in motion, and soon your partner's resentment encourages you to stay away. Pay attention to your home and try to balance your life.

WORK BALANCE

There is no such thing as a "nonworking" wife or mother. Wives work! Whether in the home for nothing or outside of it for money, they labor. Stresses occur if one marital partner expects companionship at the time the other is occupied. When both are happily engaged apart from each other, there is harmony, but when one has to stand around waiting to share leisure while the other works, anger results. Work apart... work together, but don't keep your partner on tenterhooks. Balance is essential. This applies equally to mothers preoccupied with children and housework, to ambitious career women, to working men who never come home—in short, to *all* who might ignore a waiting partner. If you must overwork for a time, make sure your spouse is warned, has something to do, and isn't angrily "hanging around" waiting for you.

To overcome the tension caused by absent husbands, couples must plan for it as much as possible. If wives have advance warning, they can do something constructive with their time and not sit around watching dinner dry out in the oven. They can work, too, or go out or see friends. It is good at times to be alone in the outside world and have fun without your spouse. Be honest about wanting a little breathing room and don't hide behind a "career." If those "I-have-to-work-late" nights mask a desire to escape your home, think about whether your marriage is going through a period of strain and why. It's quite possible that some energy is required to make your primary union more enjoyable so that work pleasure won't seem so attractive.

Certain people almost consciously try to maneuver their mates into *not* making other plans when they're working late, out of fear the partner will become involved with some activity or person outside the marriage. They prefer to have the spouse waiting, even angrily, rather than gallivanting. Don't do this! If you're making such unjust demands, maybe you are neglecting your partner and are worried about her fidelity. At such a point, don't tell your partner to twiddle her thumbs till you return. *Go home and mind your marriage*.

Home Work

At present, who does what in the home is a big problem for couples. In the past, housekeeping was clearly the woman's job, but now we are in a transition period and household roles are not so easily defined by sex. Even after a work decision is made, old attitudes may crop up and make men feel badly served and women guilty about who's going to diaper Johnny or clean the bathroom. Both partners may have equally balanced outside careers, but if they work long hours, there's bound to be trouble when they get home. Ready to relax at night, the working wife is as tired as her husband and in no mood to cook meals or run errands. Naturally, squabbles occur over who should do domestic duty, stay home to let the plumber in, do the shopping, water the plants, or take the car in for service.

Couples should be considerate of each other's jobs and of each other at home. They should not be rigidly political, maintaining an "it's-your-turn" attitude around the house. It makes for petty fights and discomforts. Commit yourself instead to trying to make your spouse's life easier, rather than proving you can get him or her to do anything. And face it—unless you have some excellent help, if you have children *one* of your jobs has to be "interruptible." It means you can't both be airline pilots flying over the middle of the Atlantic when your child develops a 105-degree fever.

CHILD REARING AND WORK

Modes of coping differ in a childless dual-career marriage, but the potential predicaments are small potatoes compared to those when there are children. A recent study in the *American Journal of Psychiatry* of twenty-eight working couples with children found that despite her career, each woman kept the primary child-rearing responsibility. These mothers were deeply concerned about their children's development and not interested in devising short cuts in child-raising techniques to help them get out of the house. When home, they were highly motivated and more likely to organize an activity with their children than twenty-four-hour-a-day mothers. They became involved in all phases of their children's lives and knew what was going on at home, in school, and on the street. If the child got sick or there was a breakdown in domestic help, it was Mom's job to straighten things out. In all twenty-eight couples, the husbands were very supportive, but the women were more *sensitive* to their children's needs and more aware of the problems as they arose. Unlike their husbands, the women suffered strain and fatigue.

To a woman, the twenty-eight believed it was not the quantity but the quality of time that counted and each tried to make every moment with children productive. To relieve the pressure, they were forced to lower career ambitions, at least temporarily, but even so there was a trace of guilt about being away from the children for any length of time. The career mothers were doing "super-woman" dual jobs quite well, but all of them had major concerns over the conflict between their careers and their offspring.

It seems to us that these concerns and fears arise in part because women are doing something different from what their mothers and grandmothers did. Mom and Granny may have worked, but in most cases not in full-fledged, high-powered careers. The fact is, women are not yet at ease in their new career-mother situations. Eventually, society will devise ways to alleviate the career-mother's problems... eventually. Fathers could conceivably become as sensitive as mothers to children's wants, day-care centers could expand into daytime "kibbutzim," women could back off from full-time, high-energy careers when children are small, or there could be a resurgence among working women of those trained to work in the home. These are some possibilities, but *at present* women with full-time careers and young children are being squeezed dry, and the marriage relationship suffers from the drought.

WHAT TO DO TILL THE ANSWER COMES

Until American society develops a new pattern of child-rearing practices for working couples, the couples must work together. Co-operation, team effort, and careful planning are of paramount importance. Husbands must pitch in or their marriages will fall apart. Besides, a father's getting to know his children and aiding

their growth are rewarding and fascinating. Child rearing
becomes boring only when it's a twenty-four-hour-a-day
"career," but if the hours are consciously and intelligently
divided by a couple, it can become a pleasure.

Day-care centers, shorter work hours, live-in help,
baby-sitters, grandparents . . . choose one of the available
forms of relief from the dual-career/child-rearing strain
and you'll both find time to enjoy your family life *and*
your career.

COMPETITION

On the home front there is also the question of dangerous
rivalry. Competition is healthy, but it can quickly turn
marriage sickly. We don't think a husband and wife
should be competing *against* each other in the career
world. It can happen unintentionally—people often meet
and marry because they share interests. Therefore many
couples *are* in the same field, but they should not be in
direct competition with each other. If both begin as
architects and one rises to design major skyscrapers while
the other does an occasional garage, the less successful
spouse will feel upset. Twinges of jealousy and inferiority
can convulse a marriage. The more successful spouse
should try to help, not by jeopardizing his or her own
career but by encouraging the partner's.

Even if they're not in the same field, when one partner
gets more money or recognition, the other may be upset.
Lingering attitudes from the past make competition
difficult to tuck into the marital bed, and when the
woman makes more money, it can become a big lump in
the mattress. Most men find that hard to take. If,
however, the wife does not bring in a large salary, then she
may be considered "less important" in the marital
partnership. Her husband may have a patronizing
attitude toward her career. *She* can stay home because her
work is "adorable," not profitable.

Men and women will help their marriages by

respecting each other's careers, whatever they are. Taking an interest in your partner's work day improves your union because it's a good way of showing you'd rather care than compete.

Share Your Career

The old adage "Man may work from sun to sun, but woman's work is never done" has little meaning in modern marriages. The office is filled with interruptions and doesn't lend itself to sustained concentration very well, so executives and career people take work home. The work day filters past 5 P.M., slips into the evening hours, and curls around leisure time.

In dual-career families it can lead to trouble if one person and not the other has a briefcase full of homework. As we have seen, the free-and-easy spouse may be anxious for the company, or just plain anxious, and doesn't want a partner who's always busy at the job. A career need not be a total encroachment on family life. To be sure, it's an activity done apart—an inherent primary source of divisiveness—but the circumstances of separateness *can* be ﾠleviated. Involving your spouse in your career, making an effort to talk about what you do even if you are sick and tired of it brings your partner into the picture. Then he or she will not be a stranger to a most vital facet of your own life. (Think back. Had baton-swinging Sam Owens taken the trouble to cultivate his wife's interest as he did his protégée's, he might have looked forward to going home and Anita might have been glad to see him.) By sharing, you may actually get good counsel; after all your spouse is *for* you. You can reveal secrets of your thinking and scheming and have the benefit of another, independent mind to help in considering courses of action.

PAY ATTENTION

In the English film *Breaking the Sound Barrier*, a test pilot succeeds in flying his plane through Mach 1, the speed of sound. (Mind you, he's been through hell, planes have cracked up right and left trying to do just that and his best friend has gone down in a terrible, shattering crash.) Elated and shaken by what he has done and lived through, he goes into the locker room and finds his wife waiting for him. She's just returned from a shopping spree and immediately begins showing him her purchases, giving him no opportunity to tell her that he has done what no man has done before and lived. Every time he starts to say, "But, darling guess what . . ." she butts in. Finally she squeals, "Oh do look at this, isn't it ridiculous?" and she claps a hat on her head. The husband stops trying to tell his news, shrugs his shoulders, and laughs with her at the silly hat. Suddenly, he bursts into tears and falls into his wife's arms. She is completely taken aback and mumbles something about, "Darling, whatever is the matter—it's just a silly hat!" It's an exquisite scene, and by the look on the wife's face you know her husband *will* get his story out and she'll listen.

Everyone must learn to pay attention and share. Momentary preoccupation with one's own doings, as illustrated in the previous scene, is perfectly human. *Never* caring or sharing is something else again—really quite *in*human and inexcusable.

While couples can learn to share careers, what happens when a career gets in the way and becomes a palpable threat to marriage?

TEMPER YOUR CAREER

There are times in a marriage when you have to check your career to keep your mate, and caring couples should be prepared to turn down career rises in favor of the marriage. A big job must be weighed against the disruption it might produce in the family. If the advancement means meetings at night, travel, being on constant call, then the job *may* have to be passed by in favor of family intimacy, and this goes for *both* partners. It's not easy to turn down opportunities. In prestigious positions, you can make things happen and have a sense of accomplishment, which is important for us goal-oriented humans. But even though promotion is a powerful lure, try not to forget your family and by all means *consult* them. Recognize that certain jobs can ride roughshod over the best intentions, and if you want a full family life, such jobs should be avoided. If you and your spouse are ambitious and it means a lot for one or both of you to be a VIP, then do it, but realize the cost and don't berate the VIP for being away—you were forewarned.

A GOOD MARRIAGE HELPS A CAREER

Keeping your marriage content is smart for business. It's a proven fact that a stable marriage aids a career. Domestic strife and divorce, far from helping people function better on their jobs, do quite the opposite. For this reason alone, it makes sense to take care of your home front and keep it steady. Look at your spouse, take the trouble to notice signs of your neglect, and if they're there, try to correct them. Protect your home life—it can be a source of lasting pleasure. Remember, work tells you what you must do; at home you are free to carry out your principles.

MAKING IT

AMERICANS ARE ADRIFT—wandering across their vast nation, not in groups but alone. Cut off from family and history, the regular rhythm of a stable society has been replaced by the jagged, aimless tempo of unrest.

Our institutions have just been through a period of turmoil. The federal government, the military, the colleges and universities, big business, the churches, and cultural institutions—all have been shaken, often violently. Old beliefs and social support systems have declined or disappeared—marriage is one of them. We don't trust our institutions and we don't trust each other. Many seem not to care or be loyal. The government cheats—so may your wife or husband. Ballplayers leave their old clubs for better deals—so may your spouse. Be tough. Get a job, tighten up, and take care of number one. Religion, parents, neighbors, employers—no one forces us to stay married and so we split—but if home isn't stable where can we feel secure?

We're "mixed up" and need something to believe in— not phony gurus or sinister pseudoreligious saviors and certainly not wars. No stern parent is around to crack the whip, so we must learn to make associations voluntarily for mutual benefit. Divorced, we are lonely, anxious, disconnected; married, we are socially secure and have our place. Family life is *the* place to start rebuilding our faith in one another.

Ignore the Message:
The Code of Selfishness

The majority of self-help books advise us not to trust anything or anyone, not to depend on the kindness of others, and to rely on ourselves. The modern self-help fable has only one moral: "Nice guys finish last." This advice is a "logical" reaction to modern American insecurity. If you can't look to God, society, or each other, you'd better look to yourself. However, counseling selfishness worsens and furthers the problems, especially in marriage. You wouldn't go to a doctor who followed books on power, success, looking out for number one and whose code of ethics was self-determined—he'd be too wrapped up in himself to honestly try to cure you. Similarly, marriage to someone who believes in nothing but Self cannot work.

Many years of active psychiatric practice, research, and teaching, conversations with psychiatrists, psychologists, and social workers in leading medical schools around the country, extensive reading of academic literature in psychiatry, psychology, anthropology, sociology, political science, history, economics, philosophy, and personal experience in the authors' own marriage, along with observation of the successful and unsuccessful unions of those we know, have led us to the inescapable conclusion that those who advise selfishness do serious harm. They don't know what people really need, they just write books.

Divorced people aren't necessarily "healthily growing"—that's a lie perpetrated by silly popsychologists of the human-potential movement. Divorced people are often lonely and suffering. The woman may work all day for money and at night care for her offspring, while her ex-husband longs for his children, home, and a sense of belonging. People like this reflect the epidemic of anxiety and depression in America today. In the *Midtown Manhattan Study*, 24 per cent of the population was found to suffer significant impairment from emotional disorder. We are inundated with Librium, Valium, alcohol, coffee, marijuana, and cigarettes. We seek psycho-therapy, TM, yoga, est, primal scream therapy, Zen, Esalen, biofeedback, gestalt, Rolfing, encounter, and hypnosis. We keep racing out the front door chasing after answers, but one of the chief reasons for our discomfort is the very thing we slam the door on: the decline of family life and the breakup of marriages.

Americans must be helped to live in warm harmony, not encouraged to throw intimacy out into the cold. We don't mean a return to old-fashioned romantic naïveté but to healthy closeness. If it doesn't happen, the disruption of family life could destroy us.

THE NUPTIAL INTERRUPTUS

Because of the changing community standards our marriages are now voluntary, not forced. In itself this may not be such a bad thing, but like children with new-found freedom, we have sometimes abused the privilege by dissolving our homes too readily and thoughtlessly. The cycle can become insidious. For whatever reason— childhood deprivation, business frustration, excessive ambition, guilt, or repressed desires—we feel anxiety or depression and we blame our partners for our own lack of happiness, growth, and fulfillment. We want to feel better, so we "divorce" ourselves from the cause. We don't see that the disintegration of family life will make us feel more isolated, depressed, frightened, adrift, and upset. The cure—divorce—makes the disease worse.

STEADY AS SHE GOES

Those who truly understand the psychological importance of home life do not treat it lightly, do not take for granted or denigrate its importance. They never dismiss as "mere habit" what is really deep emotional attachment. Too many are surprised at how badly they feel after divorce and "suddenly" miss the security they had. The person you've been with so long, whose bed and life you've shared, with whom you've fought and made up, had children, planted gardens, taken walks means more to you than you perhaps know. It's a fact—undisrupted, harmonious home life is best for your psychological and physical health. That's why in all studies in which various traumas are rated the sudden death of a spouse scores as most severe. To preserve your marriage requires sensitivity to your partner. If you, as the "books" advise, are focusing exclusively on how to make the most of *yourself*, the union will fail.

SET YOUR SIGHTS REALISTICALLY

Your marriage can get into trouble if you heed the "me" psychologists; it can also get into trouble if you follow another group, the apparent opposite of the selfish advisers. These counselors encourage you to find too much in human relationships and lead you to expect that life will always be better and better, without any reversals. These preachers insist that "Life Can Be Beautiful," and their followers get caught up in a desparate attempt to achieve the good, the better, and the elusive best in marital communication, sex, and child rearing. Inability to reach the psychological ideal causes them to falsely conclude that their marriages are failing, and the couples split because of "poor communication, nonorgasmic sex, or bad parenting."

A SENSIBLE ALTERNATIVE

We advocate realistic goals for your marital relationship. Know where you're going and who's going with you. Sometimes marriage can be improved by better communication but sometimes, "benign neglect" is indicated. If your spouse isn't feeling sexy one night, don't start talking about what bad feelings toward you underly the indifference. You'll probably just make a pest of yourself. Relax. Tomorrow or next week your partner could be in the mood. In the meantime, it's an excellent opportunity to practice benign neglect.

Marriage may ease and comfort your life, but it's not a salvation. Don't imagine that ever-increasing closeness, empathy, caring, sympathy, touching, climaxing, and sharing will provide you with a womblike retreat, a utopia of love, a nirvana of nearness...that's poppycock. Be realistic, and you can improve your marriage. We have shown you ways and have more suggestions, but don't expect miracles or you'll be doomed to disappointment. This could lead to cynicism about the real pleasures marriage provides and possibly to divorce. When you aim too high, you denigrate your union to a habit rather than enjoying it as a comfort. In your mad pursuit of perfection, don't take the simpler joys of your home for granted. That does happen sometimes, because, once awakened, the naïve become too cynical and the "brave new world" turns into "boring old hat." The pendulum swings from the romantic, church-wedding, everlasting happiness of a Hollywood film fade-out to the gloomy and unjustified forecast that joyful marriage is impossible, that by saying "I do," you passed "Go" and you're now in a jail, which, among other things, prevents self-realization. At best, holy wedlock then seems only an economic convenience, and some gloomily resign themselves to what they consider the "realistic facts" of a long union. Expecting no companionship, fun, sex, or comfort, partners ignore each other and evolve into "married splits." They put noting in emotionally and get nothing out. Others strive too hard, cling desperately to each other, talk endlessly, employ strenuous bedroom athletics, and are overly child-centered in an attempt to attain a more perfect union. Inevitably failing to achieve their unreachable goal, they too become "married splits" or in fact get a divorce.

We believe you can achieve a loving, working marriage if you are neither naïve nor cynical. The naïve want too much and the cynical not enough. You must be *enlightened*—grown up and knowledgeable, not over-anxious or overpessimistic. You must recognize what is realistically achievable in a good marriage and understand how to obtain it: by enlightened selfishness.

Enlightened Selfishness

"Enlightened selfishness" means recognizing that we need other people in order to be attached, rooted, and comfortable and to avoid isolation, loneliness, and despair. It is the knowledge that we need others for warmth, intimacy, love, and sharing, not for exploitation. It is in your interest to consider your partner's needs. *Being considerate of your partner for your own good* is the core of enlightened selfishness.

Those who understand the workings of business grasp this concept very well. If a deal is in the seller's interest as well as the buyer's, then the deal is solid; if not, suspicions arise. Similarly, marriages are most stable when each partner feels he or she is getting a good deal. If you make

your spouse feel good, he or she will return the favor,
whether it's good sex, a good meal, a nice wardrobe, a
good joke, a helping hand, an adventure . . . each partner
must get something valuable from the continued associa-
tion, almost every day! Something must make it worth
while. Religion and society do not force us to stay
together anymore, so enlightened selfishness is the only
hope for the voluntary continuation of marriage.

In a good marriage you get back what you put in;
there's a real return on your investment as well as profit
sharing. Contribute humor and you're paid back with a
smile and a joke; be interesting and your partner is
interested and stimulating in return. But deposit little and
you'll withdraw little. If you don't talk when you come
home, after a while your spouse will ignore you and leave
you to eat your food in front of the TV. If you don't touch
your partner, he or she will cease holding you. No one can
go on unilaterally for very long. Human beings require
reinforcement from each other in order to continue a
behavior, and efforts which don't produce results
invariably cease.

Enlightened selfishness makes you think about what
you want and realize that in order to get it you must also
consider what your partner wants. Pure selfishness is
self-defeating and gets partners nowhere. Be assured,
your wants will be fulfilled *only* if you take care of your
partner's in return. This may mean becoming considerate
in areas which don't come naturally. If your partner wants
you to listen to business plans or work problems you find
tedious, you'd better train yourself to look for something
worth listening to if it's important to your spouse. Failure
to listen will cause resentment, drive your partner to
others, or make him or her retaliate by not meeting some
important need of yours.

VOLUNTARY REINING-IN

"Don't Fence Me In" . . . it's characteristic of our nation to
grow, for its people to achieve full potential and to strain

against confinement. Therefore our encouraging you to practice restraint is not going to be a popular stance. It's like predicting the fall of the stock market—if you're right, no one's going to thank you. Nevertheless, we're going to advocate restraint. Reining yourself in really isn't so depressing, but it's hard to do because it requires sacrificing some immediate rewards in favor of later greater gains. It'll be easier to do if you keep in mind that the balance of permanent pleasure is more important than a temporary one-track fanatical pursuit.

Restraint must take place in all situations in which your spouse might be hurt. If you're an avid sailor, dying to talk to company about the high seas to the exclusion of your marital partner, you should resist and make sure your spouse also has a chance to converse and have a good time. Being charming and gregarious is wonderful, but you must hold back a little to give your partner an opportunity to "shine." If you are handy and see your partner struggling to fix something, don't grab the tool or start an avalanche of suggestions. The job may not be up to your high standards, but it will be done and by someone who feels a sense of accomplishment, not victimized by a put-down.

One type of voluntary reining-in, difficult but worth doing, is sexual. Pursuing outside romantic interest is exciting, fun, but potentially damaging to marriage. The disrupted home is far more painful than a little sexual self-denial. We feel a bit stuffy and severe saying this—it would be far easier to come out in favor of "healthy" adultery to heal your marriage—but most people can't handle adultery and shouldn't try. Sure, you just might be one of the select few able to juggle extramarital sex successfully—most likely, you're not.

TEAM PLAY

Everyone is capable of being a team player. Those who claim they aren't are defiant, indifferent, or unelightened. A business man realizes he can earn more money working with others, so he pitches in; a basketball player realizes his team will win more games if he passes the ball rather than trying to score by himself; and no one runs relay races solo—the baton must be passed. When it's in your self-interest to work together with your partner, you do it. Your marital team can score more points as a unit than either of you could alone. Though the struggle between "me" and "we" goes on all through marriage, partners must figure out when which mode is appropriate. One partner doing the laundry while the other cooks is more efficient than two single people who have to do both. Two cannot live quite as cheaply as one, but certainly more so than one *plus* one. Teamwork is efficient and it isn't lonely. Sharing pleasures and pains makes the former better and the latter more bearable.

Marriage is hard for Americans because we emphasize individualism so much, but not every culture is like ours. We picture the executive agonizing over difficult decisions *alone* after advisers are gone. The Japanese make group business decisions—everyone must agree and all remain together. This group ideal permeates their society. Marriage, therefore, is less strained and the divorce rate much lower than ours. Families make sure the decision is sensible and no romantic love is required to contract a marriage. Jobs of husband and wife are strictly defined, and the marital team operates in fairly smooth fashion although not necessarily closely and intimately.

American individualism emphasizes competitiveness, self-reliance, and maximum realization of potential—yet we can and do learn to surrender individual stardom for group performance. It was Houston Ground Control and the astronauts in space working together that got us to the moon, and their accomplishment is a perfect example of the individual and team performance dovetailing. To return through earth's atmosphere and land, the astronaut commander had to be a skilled pilot and completely self-reliant. Still, on a moment's notice, by command of Ground Control, he must be prepared to surrender charge of the craft and do nothing as he's guided to a landing. If individualistic, rugged military pilots can alternate self-sufficiency and total dependence in a moment, surely any of us can learn to sacrifice a little of our own ego for the good of the marital team and our own ultimate benefit.

CAPTAIN, MY CAPTAIN

Teams need leaders and couples need direction. Excessive egalitarianism at every juncture leaves them either indecisively floundering or hopelessly battling. A system must be devised to decide who does what in case of disagreement. Obviously, if one is more concerned than the other he or she makes the choice—the partner who uses the car most decides what kind to buy, the one who cooks decides the model of the refrigerator. In cases where no one deserves the final say, it's wise to take turns. If last time you visited your partner's friend or relative, this time go to yours. If your husband just bought a new suit, it's your turn for a dress. In instances where neither of you can have your way, try to accept compromise and mild disappointment cheerfully and don't get into bitter, endless wrangles.

A Marital Quiz

It really is possible to make a marriage more fun, but many couples are excessively pessimistic about bettering their situation. Any relationship can improve if you and your partner try. It's hard work and requires determination. You'll have to give up destructive defenses and risk vulnerability. You must be ready to forgive and forget old hurts and try to achieve better communication by giving clear, simple messages, by carefully heeding words, actions, and their meanings in context. Co-operate with one another and refrain from disparagement. People derive beliefs largely by observing their own behavior. If in terror of intimacy we avoid being alone with our spouses, we believe we can't. One patient was certain he could only talk to his mistress and not to his wife. He was convinced he needed a divorce because he and his wife were incompatible. After careful questioning it was determined he thought it "unfaithful" to his girl friend to converse with his wife more than absolutely necessary. The patient was instructed to talk to his wife and not tell his mistress. He had to decide for himself whether or not his wife was capable of "relating" to him before he considered the big step of "splitting." To his surprise, he found his spouse brighter and more understanding than his secret partner! He's not only still married but much happier. It's as simple as this—change your behavior and you will change your belief.

We're going to ask questions about marriage and discuss the answers with you. Don't be scared about how you'll "score"; the authors themselves found areas in their own marriage requiring improvement and expect you'll do the same. The suggestions cover points to think about that are derived from each section of this book and cover the most important areas of your union. They've been prepared with the understanding that people shouldn't just *stay* together—they should *live well* together. To do this, they shouldn't suffer the problem areas but try to overcome strife and disappointment. You can change your behavior and improve your marriage, and this list will help. It's a good idea to go over the items every year, and we suggest New Year's Day is as good a time as any. Your car rates a periodic checkup, your children get report cards, and surely your marriage is worth thinking about systematically at least once a year. Once a month would be better, but don't do it every day—that would make you one of those tedious couples who psychologize too much. Really thinking about these questions and the answers to them will make your marriage better.

Is Your Spouse Your Best Friend?

By moving away or growing apart, we usually lose touch with childhood and college chums. Your spouse moves into the vacuum and becomes your best friend, the one with whom you share your most secret thoughts and aspirations, your best and worst times, and with whom you work and play. In every friendship there are periods of strain; the best of companions occasionally disagree and fight. It's worse being angry with your spouse than with an outsider because the strain is in your own home. When it happens, don't get too upset. Be patient. The hottest anger cools with time and doesn't have to sear marriage permanently. Actually, gradual indifference and loss of friendship is worse than the occasional fight. Partners indifferent to one another are denied one of the real pleasures of life and marriage and may end up close to no one.

How do you keep a spouse's friendship? Simply by

paying attention. Don't take your partner for granted; don't be careless with your lawfully wedded friend.

Be considerate. When you meet in the evening, listen to what each other's day was like. If one of you is alone most of the time, perhaps some company for dinner would be appreciated. If you sit too much, perhaps some exercise should be scheduled. Look for obvious ways to please.

Value each other's opinion. Be kind to one another and forgive faults. Treat your spouse as you would a "distinguished stranger." It's hard to pinpoint the bad interactions in marriage since many are automatic and almost unconscious, but consider your behavior carefully and change it when necessary. Do you stay too late at the office, avoid the bed, never have interesting discussions with your spouse? If you can't spot troubles yourselves, maybe a trusted friend or relative could help. Be careful and polite, not formal or distant, and you will be able to patch up a frayed marital friendship. Since your partner knows you best and is out for your interest, it's worth doing. Being closest of friends is one of the real joys of married life.

What Are Your "Same Old Fights" About?

Write them down and then try to divide any tasks over which you constantly squabble by an agreed-to system. This will settle "dumb" fights once and for all. Such trivia as who takes out the garbage, who drives the car pool, who buys the groceries, etc., should not occasion argument. Assign marital jobs by area of interest and competency, not by sex.

Major marital fights occur for many reasons other than who will do some disagreeable task. Hurt feelings, disappointments, slights, jealousies, and cruelties—whatever the contentions, couples must know how to *negotiate.* Let's review the main points of negotiation.

1. Be present and future oriented.
2. Argue only over things which are important and capable of being resolved quickly.
3. Be specific, not vague, about what bothers you.
4. Don't bring up new points of conflict during the battle over another one.
5. Deal directly and openly with the transgression at the time it occurs or as close to the time as reasonable.
6. Don't bring up the past during a disagreement. Nothing can be done about it and it usually leads to unfortunate name-calling.
7. Contain your emotions. Do not express excessive aggression or hurt feelings. *Shut up* negative emotions in the heat of anger or desire to confess.
8. Avoid accusation, condemning your spouse, and counteraccusation.
9. Don't imply that someone else would be easier to live with.
10. Resolve the argument. Don't leave the matter hanging inconclusively over your marriage.

If you don't know how to negotiate, marriage can be an unbearable hell of indecisive, painful, ego-shattering fights or a silent empty fearful prison; either way, it's no place to be! Follow the rules and though there will still be unpleasant, angry disagreements at times, they will be quickly settled and constructive peace will reign.

Are You Both Too Predictable?

We hope the answer is no. A spouse should be reliable, but not predictable. Do different things, make changes in your life. Don't bore each other with routine—have unexpected fun. In the middle of the week, play hooky, go off somewhere for an adventure. Have guests in on week nights (it's incredible how many people only socialize on Saturday nights). Company can be a welcome change, and dinner doesn't have to be fancy especially with good friends. Maintain a fluctuating "interest level." Take time and care with your mind. Go to places you've never been before, learn something new, join an organization. Participate together in politics or charitable work. Take up a new sport, try new foods. Take time and care with your appearance. Change your hairdo, keep your figure, be attractive to one another. Have something stimulating to say but don't tell each other *everything*. Have some secrets, a private pocket in your life; a little selective personal mystery keeps partners on their toes.

Don't keep doing the same things. Repetition is as bad for you as chaos. Pretend you're trying to make an impression and be interesting as well as interested. Make your partner feel that what he or she is saying is worth being heard. It'll make your spouse feel good, and when people feel better, they try harder.

Do You Laugh Together?

We recommend it highly. Humor can do wonders for your union. It helps stifle negative emotions, while at the same time relieving tension by providing a psychological "moat" between spouses when things are too close and touchy. It can also be a show of affection, because intimacy is underscored through private "in-jokes." Most successful couples say they share laughter and use it often to get over rough spots, to play together, and to make their lives more fun. In or out of bed, it's good to laugh. If you've become too serious with each other about chores, leisure-time activities, sex, etc., it's time for a change. Don't be too angry to laugh. Laugh at yourself, at each other, and at the whole human comedy.

Do You Feel Used?

To some extent, all of us harbor scattered, mild resentments and feel we're giving more than we're getting. This is probably due to the lingering childlike wish to be taken care of that nestles deep down in everyone's psyche. We *all* feel "used" at times and shouldn't make too much fuss about it, but if it's more than an occasional feeling and you are in fact convinced you're being "had," it's very bad for marriage and should be corrected. Marriage is based on tit-for-tat, and angry, resentful "put-upons" make poor spouses. It's give and take all the way, and if your marriage is seriously unbalanced, *right* it as soon as possible. Unequal marriages do *not* work well in a democracy. Neither partner prospers when exploited, and each must give something to and get something out of the union.

Can You Make Yourself Listen
and Be Heard?

Getting through to your partner is more likely if you yourself can be gotten through to. Learn to listen carefully and to respond precisely and make sure that what you broadcast *is* what's heard. Let the rules of negotiation light up your marital radar screen. Don't be petty. Argue diplomatically and only on important matters, and pick a time when you're in control. Sometimes you have to be blunt and hurt or threaten, but use this approach rarely and only after much consideration. Don't run away from sensible confrontation; resolving disagreements is necessary and even satisfying.

Do You Have a Good Life Together
and a Good Life Apart?

Delicate balance is reached by maintaining a correct degree of interpersonal distance in marriage—too close and you feel trapped, too far and you experience neglect. Like Goldilocks in the Three Bears' cottage you're looking for "just right." Couples who are too close are not free-standing adults but intertwined infants obsessed with and too dependent upon each other. Puerile attitudes lead to painful emotions and behavior, including rage, possessiveness, jealousy, and intrusiveness. Couples too far apart are "married splits" experiencing little or no love, caring or interchange. Like hospital wards, their households are neat, polite, quiet, and sterile, but their emotional needs are not met.

In a proper marital relationship, partners don't freeze and don't smother. They realize that their best "working" distance is not fixed rigidly but constantly varying, and every so often they ask themselves if they're moving toward or away from each other. They aren't frightened by distance-versus-closeness and adjust by striving to avoid the danger zones of extremes. Too close, they seek privacy; too preoccupied, they remember to take time alone together. They are sensitive to each other's needs because they know marriage is a living institution composed of two people whose intimacy is never static. This closeness may wax and wane, but it must always be guarded.

How's Your Sex Life?

Your erotic life never stays steady. It's always changing and needs attention. That's one reason we suggest monthly or at least yearly reassessment. Even if your sex life is great now, it may be troubled next month or next year and need to be improved. Think about how often and how well you sleep together. Is there any change? Are you satisfied? If not, is this the only shared area in your life that is suffering, or is it part of a general decline in marital satisfaction? If so, it's an indicator which shows that more than your bed needs attention.

Delicate, loving, exciting sex calls for time and imagination. Too many people ignore their sex lives out of prudishness or embarrassment, and naturally their relations deteriorate. Do you give it enough thought and care? Be as considerate of sex as you are of any valued, worthwhile activity.

How Do You Present Yourself to Your Spouse?

You'll probably say "honestly," but you must realize, either consciously or unconsciously, that we *select* what we give of ourselves. For example, some women present themselves as helpless, out of fear they'll threaten their husbands by seeming "competent." Some men present themselves as all wise and incapable of error in order to "snow" their wives. The opinions formed by the spouses of scatterbrained wives and omnipotent husbands are influenced by what they're given to see.

Think, then, of the image you present to your spouse. Are you proud of it and does it allow you to derive pleasure from the marriage? If you present yourself as stupid, how can you feel like anything but a nitwit around your partner? If you appear all wise, how can you ever relax from your Olympian pose? We should not pretend too much in marriage lest it become a sham but we should remember that what we project does influence our partners! It's okay to admit failings, but not exclusively. If you talk of nothing but your shortcomings, you'll be perceived as inept, no matter how capable you are! You certainly watch your image with strangers or on the job, and it pays to do the same self-guarding at home. You'll feel better, and your partner will like you better.

What Should You Change in Yourself to Make the Marriage Better?

This question is tricky because people usually think in terms of their partner's changing. Turn your thinking inward—it's worth the effort. Changing your actions is as hard as changing your golf swing, tennis stroke, or the way you throw a ball, but keep at it. Pick something your consort agrees *needs* changing and which *can* be altered. Probably it will be difficult at first, and you'll feel awkward and phony, but it's worth pursuing. Constructive variations in behavior can change your outlook from gloomy despair to hope and inspire you to make still other modifications. Little by little you'll feel happier with your home life.

What Should Your Partner Change to Satisfy You?

If you can't think of anything, hooray for you! It's wise to make the most of your marital partner's assets and minimize liabilities. If your wife is a wonderful friend, mother, companion but a little inhibited in bed, try to improve things. But if you can't, concentrate on her good points. If your husband is brilliant in conversation and loves to do most of the things you do but isn't handy around the house, stop berating him and hire a handy man.

Remember, too, that if you're dissatisfied, it could be other than your partner's fault. It may in fact be *you*, or maybe it's the "world" or just plain "bad luck." People are often unhappy because of poor health, no money, or unrewarding jobs and unthinkingly take it out on their mates. Stop and ask yourself if there isn't some other reason why you're yelling. It could save you a lot of grief.

What Do You Like Best About Your Partner?

Whatever it is, tell your spouse *often*. Lots of couples take each other's good points for granted and concentrate on faults. Don't be a perfectionist and tear the other down, or you may wind up appreciating each other . . . too late. In *The Birthmark*, Nathaniel Hawthorne told the story of a man married to a woman lovely in all ways except for a small purple blemish on her face. The mark became an obsession with the husband who wanted her beauty perfect. In attempting to erase the mark, he succeeded in destroying his wife. If the husband had only concentrated on his wife's good points instead of her one small flaw, the couple could have enjoyed married life. Remember this the next time you're ready to zero in on your spouse's failings.

What's Something New and Interesting You Could Do Together This Year?

Don't try to defend what you have been doing just because you've been doing it year after year. Corporations that do this eventually fold—similarly your marriage could collapse from lack of growth. Expand your horizons, grow together, seek new occasions, and you'll delight in each other anew. Thinking this way injects a spirit of adventure and fun into your marriage. Renewed and refreshed, you embark on something different and enjoy each other as you discover knowledge, places, or activities as a team.

How Are You at Controlling Your Temper?

Marriage is a temple, not an arena. It's an art, a learned skill, not a place to relax and let everything including your deepest rage "hang out." In the art of marriage, head-on collisions should be avoided. After all, you're not riding around in "bumper cars" trying to jolt somebody. Shrewd, undetected flattery should be employed to make your mate feel good. Diplomacy prevents war and requires careful phrasing and attention to the possible reactions of others. Before you blurt out the Whole Truth, consider this: even if you feel better, will your spouse? Think of the effect of your words before uttering them and you may decide to *shut up*.

Are You Jealous?

Everyone is, sometimes. We fear our mates are attracted to persons outside the marriage or that people like our mates better than us and wouldn't associate with us otherwise. Jealousy is a normal reaction when we're threatened with the loss of a valued person or when someone outshines us and takes away the love and admiration we seek. The more secure you are within yourself, the less jealousy you'll experience. If you feel you deserve your partner, you won't fear losing the relationship.

Since everyone feels jealous at times, it's best to tolerate, control, and not make too much of this painful state. Jealous behavior alienates couples and can bring about the thing most feared—loss of the partner. Someone who becomes too intrusive and attempts to invade his or her spouse's privacy makes a big mistake. It's much wiser to allow your marital partner freedom and to respect his or her individuality, just as yours must be respected. If your spouse is curious, remember that it's normal to ask, "Who was that on the phone?" or "Where did you go this afternoon?" Don't become defensive and secretive, but if your mate begins to oversnoop, you'll have to put a stop to it.

Jealousy also serves as a warning signal. If you fear you're losing a partner, it may mean your spouse requires more attention from you or perhaps needs to be reassured. Heed your internal apprehension and act carefully to correct the danger.

Jealousy is painful, but it's also a sign of caring. If you never feel it, you either don't care very much or you're too secure. Jealousy livens things up and makes spouses pay attention to each other. Some is good for everyone.

Are You Getting a Good Deal?

You oughta be! If you agree on common goals and are progressing toward them while living together with tolerance, respect, honesty, pleasure, and humor, and if you are best of friends, preferring each other's company to all others, and help, support, soothe, and stimulate one another, you certainly *do* have a very good deal.

Pay attention to these questions and their answers, and your marriage will improve, but remember, don't expect immediate miracles. It's hard to change marital patterns, and doing so often calls for more effort and attention than impatient couples are willing to give. Try again and again to bring spirit into your home and make your marriage a pleasurable success.

Family Centers

Home shouldn't be a "safe house" into which you scuttle and hide. It's a lot more than a refuge; it's a place of support where the marital team produces more than any of its members could alone. It's a dynamic laboratory of social change where generations clash, stimulate, and educate each other. There are no advertisements or neon signs telling you the family center is the place to be, but when homelife is good, there's no need to look elsewhere.

EXTRAMARITAL LIFE

No matter how much they try to shut it out, sooner or later all married partners must deal with the outside world. Everyone feels a constant tension between the wish to be with others when alone and to be alone when with others. Those who like to be alone too much can have lonely, neglected mates. Whenever a spouse desires to do something away from the partner, the independent activity can *imply* rejection and abandonment. The partner who is left feels less threatened if the one leaving is *forced* to go (work) rather than *wants* to (play). The most intimidating outside activity is friendship with the opposite sex, an increasing and fairly new phenomenon. For generations, aside from relatives the only adult male a woman saw alone without her husband was a repairman, postman, milkman, or any "man" with a utilitarian prefix. Nowadays she may see old schoolmates, business associates, even former lovers, and enjoy their company. We feel friends of the opposite sex are good for all as well as essential to some marrieds. It helps keep a person from feeling trapped and tied down, but it does risk the jealousy of the spouse.

Next in order of threat are friends of the same sex. They too can cause fits of jealousy and feelings of rejection in the partner. At times people prefer to be with their chums and this can be a big problem if they work long hours, have limited free time, and are spending it away from their spouses. Again, you have to use common sense and not try to get away with excessive absenteeism.

It's wise to permit your partner independent acts as cheerfully as possible but be prepared to go ahead even if your spouse is resentful. Those who can't take any irritation become the prisoners of their partners' whims. If you want to go to a dinner alone with a friend once in a while, your mate may get irritated and jealous, but don't fall apart—you have a right to "time off." This also applies to golf, tennis, poker, bowling, sailing, and skiing. As long as you don't *abuse* the privilege, you ought to go if it will make you happy. Accept your consort's long face; it's probably momentary pique and soon forgotten.

While "business" is a convenient excuse, we suggest you not abuse this privilege either. In order to get away from a spouse, it's tempting to blame a need to work and avoid implying there's something better to do. Some people schedule an "evening dinner meeting" to get them smoothly out of the house. Sociobusiness ploys like this may circumvent an immediate bad reaction but can engender long-range neglect, loneliness, and upset in partners left at home. It's not smart to use a "gray-flannel" excuse too often to get out of the house.

In-laws are a major outside force on the marriage. If your partner doesn't like your family (or vice versa), see them alone but be careful about how often. Your spouse may not feel especially rejected, believing you have to and should go, but excessive in-law involvement can strain and just about wreck a marriage. If you care about your home, you must handle your parents and relatives with kid gloves.

In all outside/inside decisions consider your partner. Don't take him or her for granted, and remember that by allowing your spouse independent acts and tolerating some feelings of jealousy and neglect, you buy your own freedom.

CONTINUITY

There is a great longing in Americans for a sense of belonging, identity, and continuity with the past. We pay exorbitant sums for old comic books, magazines, or baseball cards. We run to old movies, collect antiques, and snatch at bits of nostalgia. We search our family trees, and if we can pinpoint the place, we travel to where our ancestors were born. We read books about our old neighborhoods, which too often no longer exist. We're overwhelmed by the desire to belong and yet we have a crazy, escalating divorce rate. We tear apart our families at the same time that we crave them desperately. This is madness.

Don't split. Don't break up your marriage in some dizzy attempt to grow. Grow by all means, but don't expect thoughtless impulsive splitting to foster growth. In most cases, your partner didn't stunt you—it's either your own fault or the result of circumstances beyond either of your controls.

Develop within the framework of your marriage. If you've given over certain duties to your partner and no longer know how to do them, then *learn*. Don't split over them. Fear of dependency and helplessness will be cured by knowledge and self-reliance, not by running away.

Order, security, and reliability are neither bad nor boring. They leave you free for creativity and growth. If there is something you want to do, arrange to do it. If your partner finds it hard to adjust to your new ways, be tolerant. Don't give up change, but help your spouse to accept it. If you have to, live with your partner's disapproval for a time, don't use it as an excuse to do nothing and then impulsively split. You and your partner have been through much together, and if there are children, they are your link to the future, a modest and proper bid for immortality. Don't throw it away.

In one sense, it's a good thing that marriages are no longer automatically "till death do us part." It means we cannot take anything for granted. We must work for the common good of marriages, and this could result in their becoming better than they've ever been before. We're living through a transition period in American social history—the old order has scarcely changed before a new one takes hold. The divorce rate, while still rising, is doing so more slowly, and we anticipate that it will begin to fall. We hope this book will help speed up the decline of divorce—it will, if you do your part.